SOUPS & STEWS

**BARNES
&NOBLE
BOOKS**
NEW YORK

Pictured on front cover:

Fresh Tomato Soup, *page 127*

Previously published as
Better Homes and Gardens® Cooking for Today Soups & Stews

Copyright © 2004, 1993 by Meredith Corporation, Des Moines, Iowa. First Edition.

This edition published for Barnes & Noble, Inc., by Meredith Books.

Printed in China

ISBN: 0-7607-6039-X

On a snow-drifted February night we call them "chill-chasing" and "rib-sticking." On the hottest day of July we refer to them as "refreshing" and "cooling." And other times, they're simply "satisfying" and "great-tasting."

No matter what the season, this book is filled with dozens of soups to suit your needs. There are soups filled with meat, poultry, fish, seafood, vegetables, cheese, beans, and lentils. There are soups that simmer on the stovetop all day so their flavors blend and build and speedy soups that can be ready in less than an hour (and some in less than 30 minutes).

There are thick and rich bisques and stocky, nourishing chowders. There are zesty chilies with and without beans, ranging from mild to extra-spicy in flavor. There are stews so thick you can eat them with a fork and chilled soups that go hand-in-hand with lazy summer meals.

Most of these soups are meant to be the star of your meal, but there are also soups to serve as a taste-tempting opener for a meal and even soups to serve in place of dessert.

So reach for your soup kettle and make soup tonight. Then ladle up a bowlful of the ultimate comfort food.

CONTENTS

BROTH SUBSTITUTIONS

When you're in a hurry and don't have time to make your own home-made broth, try one of these convenience products: ready-to-use canned beef or chicken broth, canned condensed beef or chicken broth, or instant beef, chicken, or vegetable bouillon granules or cubes. Mix both the canned condensed broth and bouillon granules or cubes according to package directions before using.

CLARIFYING BROTH

For crystal-clear soups, use broth that's been clarified. First, separate an egg, saving the yolk for another use. In a Dutch oven or kettle combine your strained broth, ¼ cup cold water, and the egg white. Bring to boiling. Remove from heat and let stand for 5 minutes. Strain the broth through a large sieve or colander lined with several layers of damp, 100% cotton cheesecloth.

KEEP IT HOT OR KEEP IT COLD

Serve soup at just the right temperature by heating or chilling the individual bowls. Run the bowls under hot tap water to heat them. Or, chill them in the refrigerator for icy cold soups.

CHILI POWDER

Chili powder is a ground blend of relatively mild chili peppers, oregano, cumin, garlic, and sometimes salt. Chili powders range in color from bright red to dark red, depending on the chili pepper used. Because every brand will have its own combination of spices, it's best to experiment till you find your favorite. Store chili powder in the refrigerator; it will hold its color and keep its flavor longer.

LENTILS

Lentils are tiny, brownish green, disk-shaped, dried seeds that are members of the legume family. Lentils are a source of vegetable protein. Cooked lentils have a beanlike texture and a mild, nutty flavor. There is no need to soak lentils before cooking—they become tender in about 20 minutes (slightly longer if cooked in a tomato mixture).

Lentils are widely available and should be stored, tightly covered, in a cool, dry place for up to 1 year.

HEALTH CONSCIOUS SOUPS

To reduce fat and calories in homemade soups, try these tips:

■ Instead of thickening soup with a fat and flour roux or flour and water, puree one or more of the vegetables and return the puree to the soup. Instant mashed potato flakes also work well.

■ To remove excess fat from soup, cover and chill it overnight or until the fat solidifies on the surface of the soup. Then lift off the fat and discard it.

BEEF BROTH

4   pounds meaty beef soupbones (shank
      crosscuts, short ribs, *or* arm bones)
3   carrots, cut up
2   medium onions, cut up
2   stalks celery with leaves, cut up
8   sprigs parsley
10   whole black peppers
4   bay leaves
1   tablespoon dried basil *or* thyme,
      crushed
2   cloves garlic, halved
1   teaspoon salt

Place soupbones in a large shallow roasting pan. Bake in a 450° oven about 30 minutes or till well browned, turning once. Place soupbones in a large Dutch oven. Pour ½ cup *water* into the roasting pan, scraping up crusty browned bits. Add water mixture to Dutch oven. Add carrots, onions, celery, parsley, peppers, bay leaves, basil, garlic, salt, and 10 cups water. Bring to boiling; reduce heat. Cover and simmer 3½ hours. Remove soupbones.

Pour broth through a large sieve or colander lined with 2 layers of cheesecloth. Discard vegetables and seasonings. If desired, clarify broth (see tip, page 4). If using the broth while hot, skim fat. (Or chill broth, then lift off fat.) If desired, when bones are cool enough to handle, remove meat from bones and reserve meat for another use. Discard bones. Store broth and reserved meat, if any, in *separate* covered containers in the refrigerator up to 3 days or in the freezer up to 6 months. Makes about 8 cups broth.

CHICKEN BROTH

For richer color, use an unpeeled yellow onion.

2½ pounds bony chicken pieces (backs, necks, and wings from 2 chickens)
3 stalks celery with leaves, cut up
2 carrots, cut up
1 large onion, cut up
2 sprigs parsley
1 teaspoon salt
½ teaspoon dried thyme, sage, *or* basil, crushed
¼ teaspoon pepper
2 bay leaves
6 cups cold water

In a large Dutch oven or kettle place chicken pieces; celery; carrots; onion; parsley; salt; thyme, sage, or basil; pepper; and bay leaves. Add water. Bring to boiling; reduce heat. Cover and simmer for 2 hours. Remove chicken.

To strain, pour broth through a large sieve or colander lined with 2 layers of cheesecloth. Discard vegetables and seasonings. If desired, clarify broth (see tip, page 4). If using the broth while hot, skim fat. (Or chill broth, then lift off fat.) If desired, when bones are cool enough to handle, remove meat from bones and reserve meat for another use. Discard bones. Store broth and reserved meat, if any, in *separate* covered containers in the refrigerator up to 3 days or in the freezer up to 6 months. Makes about 5 cups broth and 2½ cups meat.

Crockery-cooker directions: In a 3½- or 4-quart electric crockery cooker combine chicken pieces; celery; carrots; onion; parsley; salt; thyme, sage, or basil; pepper; bay leaves; and *4 cups* water. Cover and cook on low-heat setting for 8 to 10 hours. Remove chicken. Strain and store broth and meat as above.

HEARTLAND STEAK AND VEGETABLE SOUP

A big bowl of this rib-sticking soup and a loaf of crusty French bread are all you need for supper on a cold, January night.

2   4-ounce beef cubed steaks
¼   teaspoon garlic salt
⅛   teaspoon pepper
1   tablespoon cooking oil
⅓   cup margarine *or* butter
½   cup chopped onion
½   cup chopped carrot
½   cup chopped celery
½   cup frozen baby lima beans
½   cup all-purpose flour
4   cups water
1   7½-ounce can tomatoes, cut up
½   cup frozen whole kernel corn
½   cup frozen peas
1   tablespoon snipped fresh basil *or*
        1 teaspoon dried basil, crushed
2   teaspoons instant beef bouillon
        granules
2   teaspoons Worcestershire sauce

Sprinkle steaks with garlic salt and pepper. In a 4-quart Dutch oven cook steaks in hot oil about 3 minutes or till done, turning once. Remove steaks from pan and cut into cubes; set meat aside. Drain fat from pan.

In the same pan melt margarine or butter. Add onion, carrot, celery, and lima beans. Cook and stir till onion is tender. Stir in flour. Stir water into flour mixture all at once. Cook and stir till thickened and bubbly. Stir in *undrained* tomatoes, corn, peas, basil, bouillon granules, Worcestershire sauce, and cubed meat. Return to boiling. Reduce heat and simmer, covered, about 5 minutes or till heated through. Makes 4 servings.

Nutrition information per serving: 384 calories, 20 g protein, 29 g carbohydrate, 22 g fat (4 g saturated), 36 mg cholesterol, 933 mg sodium, 611 mg potassium.

MEATBALL SOUP
A full-flavored Italian specialty featuring pasta, garbanzo beans, and spinach.

1   beaten egg
½   cup soft bread crumbs (⅔ slice)
2   tablespoons grated Parmesan *or*
        Romano cheese
1   tablespoon snipped fresh parsley
1   tablespoon finely chopped onion
¼   teaspoon garlic salt
⅛   teaspoon pepper
½   pound ground beef
1   15-ounce can garbanzo beans, rinsed
        and drained
1   14½-ounce can beef broth
1   14½-ounce can Italian-style stewed
        tomatoes
1½   cups water
1   cup sliced fresh mushrooms
1   teaspoon dried Italian seasoning,
        crushed
¼   cup tiny bow-tie pasta *or* ditalini
3   cups torn spinach *or* ½ of a 10-ounce
        package frozen chopped spinach,
        thawed and well drained

In a medium mixing bowl combine egg, bread crumbs, Parmesan or Romano cheese, parsley, onion, garlic salt, and pepper. Add ground beef; mix well. Shape meat mixture into 36 balls.

In a large skillet cook meatballs over medium heat about 8 minutes or till no pink remains, turning occasionally to brown evenly. Drain fat from pan. Set meatballs aside.

In a large saucepan stir together garbanzo beans, beef broth, *undrained* tomatoes, water, mushrooms, and Italian seasoning. Bring to boiling. Add pasta. Return to boiling. Reduce heat and simmer, covered, for 10 to 12 minutes or till pasta is tender. Stir in spinach and meatballs. Cook for 1 to 2 minutes more or just till spinach is wilted. Makes 4 servings.

Nutrition information per serving: 323 calories, 23 g protein, 36 g carbohydrate, 10 g fat (4 g saturated), 91 mg cholesterol, 1,251 mg sodium, 962 mg potassium.

EASY HAMBURGER-VEGETABLE SOUP

Sprinkle the crispy cheesy cracker topping on any of your favorite soups, stews, or chilies.

1   pound ground beef *or* ground pork
½   cup chopped onion
½   cup chopped green pepper
4   cups beef broth
1   cup frozen whole kernel corn
1   7½-ounce can tomatoes, cut up
½   of a 9-ounce package frozen
    lima beans
½   cup chopped, peeled potato *or*
    ½ cup loose-pack frozen hash
    brown potatoes
1   medium carrot, cut into julienne
    strips (½ cup)
1   tablespoon snipped fresh basil *or*
    1 teaspoon dried basil, crushed
1   teaspoon Worcestershire sauce
⅛   teaspoon pepper
1   bay leaf
    Cracker Mix (optional)

In a large saucepan or Dutch oven cook ground beef or pork, onion, and green pepper till meat is brown and onion is tender. Drain fat from pan. Stir in beef broth, corn, *undrained* tomatoes, lima beans, potato, carrot, basil, Worcestershire sauce, pepper, and bay leaf. Bring to boiling. Reduce heat and simmer, covered, for 15 to 20 minutes or till vegetables are tender. Discard bay leaf. If desired, top each serving with *¼ cup* of the Cracker Mix. Makes 4 servings.

Nutrition information per serving: 309 calories, 28 g protein, 25 g carbohydrate, 12 g fat (5 g saturated), 71 mg cholesterol, 958 mg sodium, 784 mg potassium.

Cracker Mix: In a large bowl combine 1 cup *bite-size fish-shape pretzel or cheese-flavored crackers,* 1 cup *oyster crackers,* 1 cup *bite-size shredded wheat biscuits,* and 1 cup *miniature rich round crackers.* In a small bowl combine 2 tablespoons *cooking oil,* ½ teaspoon *Worcestershire sauce,* ⅛ teaspoon *garlic powder,* and dash *bottled hot pepper sauce;* pour over cracker mixture, tossing to coat. Sprinkle cracker mixture with 2 tablespoons grated *Parmesan cheese;* toss to coat. Spread mixture on a shallow baking sheet. Bake in a 300° oven for 10 to 15 minutes or till golden, stirring once. Cool completely. Store in an airtight container. Makes about 4 cups.

Nutrition information per serving: 129 calories, 5 g protein, 16 g carbohydrate, 5 g fat (1 g saturated), 1 mg cholesterol, 110 mg sodium, 144 mg potassium.

BEEFY VEGETABLE SOUP

This colorful soup starts with a less expensive meat cut, but turns out a hearty soup loaded with flavor.

3 pounds beef shank crosscuts
3 cups water
2 teaspoons instant beef bouillon
    granules
1½ teaspoons salt
¼ teaspoon pepper
    Bouquet Garni
2 cups chopped, peeled tomatoes *or*
    one 16-ounce can tomatoes, cut up
1½ cups peeled sweet potatoes cut into
    ¾-inch cubes
1 cup parsnips cut into ½-inch pieces
1 cup sliced carrot
1 cup sliced celery
2 cups fresh pea pods, halved crosswise
    or one 6-ounce package frozen pea
    pods, thawed and halved crosswise

Trim fat from beef shanks. In a large Dutch oven or kettle combine meat, water, bouillon granules, salt, and pepper. Prepare Bouquet Garni; add to Dutch oven. Bring to boiling. Reduce heat and simmer, covered, for 2 hours.

Remove meat from soup; set aside to cool. Cut meat off bones and coarsely chop; discard bones. Skim fat from broth. Stir chopped meat, chopped tomatoes or *undrained* canned tomatoes, sweet potatoes, parsnips, carrot, and celery into broth.

Return to boiling. Reduce heat and simmer, covered, for 15 minutes. Stir in pea pods; simmer, covered, for 1 to 2 minutes more or till the pea pods are crisp-tender. Remove Bouquet Garni and discard. Makes 6 servings.

Bouquet Garni: Place 4 sprigs *parsley; leaves from 3 stalks celery;* 2 *bay leaves;* 2 cloves *garlic,* halved; and 4 sprigs fresh *thyme* or 2 teaspoons dried thyme on a 10-inch-square double thickness of *100% cotton* cheesecloth. Tie into a bag with a clean string.

Nutrition information per serving: 264 calories, 30 g protein, 24 g carbohydrate, 6 g fat (2 g saturated), 59 mg cholesterol, 929 mg sodium, 962 mg potassium.

LAMB AND ORZO SOUP WITH SPINACH

Orzo, also called rosamarina, is a tiny pasta shaped like long grains of rice.

2½ pounds lamb shanks
4 cups water
4 cups chicken broth *or* vegetable broth
2 bay leaves
1 tablespoon snipped fresh oregano *or*
    1 teaspoon dried oregano, crushed
1½ teaspoons snipped fresh marjoram *or*
    ½ teaspoon dried marjoram,
    crushed
½ teaspoon salt
¼ teaspoon pepper
2 carrots, cut into julienne strips
    (1 cup)
1 cup sliced celery
¾ cup orzo (rosamarina)
3 cups torn spinach *or* ½ of a 10-ounce
    package frozen chopped spinach,
    thawed and well drained
  Finely shredded Parmesan cheese
    (optional)
  Sliced ripe olives (optional)

In a large Dutch oven or kettle combine lamb shanks, water, chicken or vegetable broth, bay leaves, oregano, marjoram, salt, and pepper. Bring to boiling. Reduce heat and simmer, covered, for 1¼ to 1½ hours or till meat is tender.

Remove meat from soup; set aside to cool. Strain broth through a large sieve or colander lined with 2 layers of *100% cotton* cheesecloth; discard herbs. Skim fat and return broth to Dutch oven. Cut meat off bones and coarsely chop meat; discard bones.

Stir chopped meat, carrots, celery, and orzo into soup. Return to boiling. Reduce heat and simmer, covered, about 15 minutes or till vegetables and orzo are tender. Stir in spinach. Cook for 1 to 2 minutes more or just till spinach wilts. If desired, serve with Parmesan cheese and ripe olives. Makes 6 servings.

Nutrition information per serving: 226 calories, 25 g protein, 20 g carbohydrate, 5 g fat (2 g saturated), 59 mg cholesterol, 797 mg sodium, 579 mg potassium.

TUSCAN SAUSAGE AND BEAN SOUP

By using the crockery cooker method, you can have a dynamite dinner ready when you step in the door, even if you were on the go all day.

1¼ cups dry great northern beans
1¾ cups beef broth
½ cup chopped onion
1 clove garlic, minced
½ teaspoon dried Italian seasoning, crushed
¾ pound fresh Italian sausage links, cut into ½-inch slices
1 medium yellow summer squash *or* zucchini, sliced (2 cups)
1 14½-ounce can Italian-style tomatoes, cut up
⅓ cup dry red wine *or* water
½ of a 10-ounce package frozen chopped spinach, thawed and well drained
   Grated Parmesan cheese (optional)

Rinse beans. In a large saucepan or Dutch oven combine beans and 4 cups *cold water.* Bring to boiling. Reduce heat and simmer for 2 minutes. Remove from heat. Cover and let stand 1 hour. (Or, skip the boiling water and soak beans overnight in a covered pan.) Drain and rinse beans.

In the same pan combine beans, 4 cups fresh *water,* beef broth, onion, garlic, and Italian seasoning. Bring to boiling. Reduce heat and simmer, covered, for 2 hours or till beans are tender.

Meanwhile, in a medium skillet cook Italian sausage till brown. Drain well on paper towels. Add cooked and drained sausage, summer squash or zucchini, *undrained* tomatoes, and wine or water to bean mixture. Bring to boiling. Reduce heat and simmer, covered, about 5 minutes more or till squash is tender.

Stir in spinach. Heat through. If desired, sprinkle each serving with Parmesan cheese. Makes 4 or 5 servings.

Crockery cooker directions: Rinse beans. In a large saucepan or Dutch oven combine beans and 4 cups cold water. Boil, uncovered, for 10 minutes; drain. Prepare sausage as directed above. In a 3½- or 4-quart crockery cooker combine the drained beans, 4 cups fresh *water,* beef broth, onion, garlic, Italian seasoning, cooked and drained Italian sausage, squash or zucchini, *undrained* tomatoes, and red wine or water. Cook, covered, on low heat setting for 11 to 12 hours or till beans are tender. Just before serving, stir spinach into soup. If desired, sprinkle each serving with Parmesan cheese.

Nutrition information per serving: 563 calories, 36 g protein, 63 g carbohydrate, 19 g fat (6 g saturated), 49 mg cholesterol, 1,155 mg sodium, 1,799 mg potassium.

SAUSAGE-VEGETABLE SOUP

Basil, onion, garlic, and Parmesan cheese combine to give an Italian flavor to this simple-to-make soup.

¾ pound bulk Italian sausage
½ cup chopped onion
3 cups beef broth
1 14½-ounce can Italian-style tomatoes, cut up
1 cup thinly sliced carrot
1 tablespoon snipped fresh basil *or* 1 teaspoon dried basil, crushed
1 tablespoon snipped fresh parsley
2 cloves garlic, minced
⅛ teaspoon pepper
1 cup sliced zucchini *or* yellow summer squash
1 cup rotini *or* small shell macaroni
¼ cup grated Parmesan cheese

In a large saucepan or Dutch oven cook Italian sausage and onion till sausage is no longer pink and onion is tender. Pour sausage mixture into a colander to drain off fat; rinse meat and drain again. Return sausage mixture to saucepan or Dutch oven and stir in beef broth, *undrained* tomatoes, carrot, basil, parsley, garlic, and pepper.

Bring to boiling. Reduce heat and simmer, covered, for 10 minutes. Stir in zucchini or yellow summer squash and rotini or small shell macaroni.

Return to boiling. Reduce heat and simmer, covered, for 10 to 15 minutes more or till macaroni and vegetables are tender. Sprinkle each serving with Parmesan cheese. Makes 4 servings.

Nutrition information per serving: 406 calories, 23 g protein, 35 g carbohydrate, 19 g fat (7 g saturated), 54 mg cholesterol, 1,483 mg sodium, 772 mg potassium.

HAM AND BEAN SOUP WITH VEGETABLES

Comfort food! Ham and bean soup takes on a new look with the colorful addition of parsnips, carrots, and spinach.

1 cup dry navy beans
1¼ to 1½ pounds meaty smoked pork hocks *or* one 1- to 1½-pound meaty ham bone
1 cup chopped onion
½ cup sliced celery
1 tablespoon instant chicken bouillon granules
1 tablespoon snipped fresh parsley
1 tablespoon snipped fresh thyme *or* 1 teaspoon dried thyme, crushed
¼ teaspoon pepper
2 cups chopped parsnips *or* rutabaga
1 cup sliced carrots
1 10-ounce package frozen chopped spinach, thawed and well drained

Rinse beans. In a Dutch oven combine beans and 5 cups *cold water.* Bring to boiling. Reduce heat and simmer, uncovered, for 2 minutes. Remove from heat. Cover and let stand 1 hour. (Or, skip boiling water and soak beans overnight in a covered pan.) Drain and rinse beans.

In the same pan combine beans, 5 cups fresh *water,* pork hocks or ham bone, onion, celery, bouillon granules, parsley, thyme, and pepper. Bring to boiling. Reduce heat and simmer, covered, for 1¾ hours. Remove pork hocks or ham bone; set aside to cool. Mash beans slightly. Stir in parsnips or rutabaga and carrots. Return to boiling. Reduce heat and simmer, covered, about 15 minutes or till vegetables are tender.

Meanwhile, cut meat off bones and coarsely chop. Discard bones. Stir meat and spinach into saucepan. Cook till heated through. Makes 4 or 5 servings.

Nutrition information per serving: 347 calories, 23 g protein, 60 g carbohydrate, 3 g fat (1 g saturated), 19 mg cholesterol, 1,175 mg sodium, 1,228 mg potassium.

TOMATO-SPLIT PEA SOUP

The split peas and pork hocks make this a filling and nutritious entreé that won't burden your budget.

1   cup dry split yellow *or* green peas
1¼ to 1½ pounds meaty smoked pork
       hocks *or* one 1- to 1½-pound meaty
       ham bone
4½ cups chicken broth *or* vegetable broth
½   of a 6-ounce can (⅓ cup) tomato paste
¾   teaspoon snipped fresh tarragon *or*
       ¼ teaspoon dried tarragon, crushed
¼   teaspoon pepper
1   bay leaf
1   cup sliced carrot
1   cup chopped celery
½   cup chopped onion
1   cup Cracker Mix (optional)
       (see recipe, page 12)

Rinse peas. In a large saucepan or Dutch oven combine peas, pork hocks or ham bone, chicken or vegetable broth, tomato paste, tarragon, pepper, and bay leaf. Bring to boiling. Reduce heat and simmer, covered, for 1 hour. Remove pork hocks or ham bone; set aside to cool.

Stir carrot, celery, and onion into saucepan. Return to boiling. Reduce heat and simmer, covered, for 20 to 30 minutes or till vegetables are tender.

Meanwhile, cut meat off bones and coarsely chop meat. Discard the bones. Stir the meat into saucepan. Cook till heated through. Discard the bay leaf. If desired, sprinkle each serving with ¼ cup Cracker Mix. Makes 4 servings.

Nutrition information per serving: 310 calories, 27 g protein, 42 g carbohydrate, 4 g fat (1 g saturated), 19 mg cholesterol, 1,365 mg sodium, 1,224 mg potassium.

CLASSIC CHICKEN-SAUSAGE GUMBO

Filé (fee LAY) powder is ground sassafras leaves that Cajun cooks use to thicken and add a thymelike flavor to gumbos. Because it gets stringy when it's boiled, pass it at the table and let each person add his own.

⅓ cup all-purpose flour
¼ cup cooking oil
½ cup chopped onion
½ cup chopped celery
½ cup chopped green pepper
4 cloves garlic, minced
¼ teaspoon black pepper
¼ teaspoon ground red pepper
3 cups chicken broth, heated
1½ cups chopped cooked chicken *or* turkey
8 ounces andouille sausage *or* fully cooked smoked sausage links, halved lengthwise and cut into ½-inch slices
1½ cups sliced okra *or* one 10-ounce package frozen cut okra
2 bay leaves
3 cups hot cooked rice
   Filé powder (optional)

For roux, in a large heavy saucepan or Dutch oven combine flour and oil till smooth. Cook over medium-high heat for 5 minutes, stirring constantly. Reduce heat to medium. Cook and stir about 15 minutes or till roux is dark reddish brown.

Stir in onion, celery, green pepper, garlic, black pepper, and ground red pepper. Cook over medium heat for 3 to 5 minutes or till vegetables are just crisp-tender, stirring often.

Gradually stir in hot chicken broth, chicken or turkey, sausage, okra, and bay leaves. Bring to boiling. Reduce heat and simmer, covered, about 15 minutes or till okra is tender. Discard bay leaves. Serve in bowls with rice.

If desired, serve with ¼ to ½ teaspoon filé powder to stir into each serving. Makes 4 servings.

Nutrition information per serving: 614 calories, 37 g protein, 61 g carbohydrate, 24 g fat (5 g saturated), 87 mg cholesterol, 1,129 mg sodium, 774 mg potassium.

CHICKEN SOUP WITH LENTILS AND BARLEY

The lentils and barley give this pleasing poultry soup an earthy, down-home flavor.

½   cup dry lentils
1   cup sliced leeks *or* chopped onion
½   cup chopped sweet red *or* green
      pepper
1   clove garlic, minced
2   tablespoons margarine *or* butter
5   cups chicken broth
1½ teaspoons snipped fresh basil *or*
      ½ teaspoon dried basil, crushed
1   teaspoon snipped fresh oregano *or*
      ¼ teaspoon dried oregano, crushed
¾   teaspoon snipped fresh rosemary *or*
      ¼ teaspoon dried rosemary, crushed
¼   teaspoon pepper
1½ cups chopped cooked chicken *or*
      turkey
1½ cups sliced carrots
½   cup quick-cooking barley
1   16-ounce can tomatoes, cut up

Rinse and drain lentils; set aside. In a large saucepan or Dutch oven cook leeks or onion, sweet red or green pepper, and garlic in margarine or butter till tender but not brown. Carefully stir in chicken broth, basil, oregano, rosemary, pepper, and the lentils. Bring to boiling. Reduce heat and simmer, covered, for 20 minutes.

Stir in chicken or turkey, carrots, and uncooked barley. Simmer, covered, about 20 minutes more or just till carrots are tender. Stir in *undrained* tomatoes; heat through. Makes 4 to 6 servings.

Nutrition information per serving: 367 calories, 28 g protein, 36 g carbohydrate, 13 g fat (3 g saturated), 51 mg cholesterol, 1,324 mg sodium, 933 mg potassium.

ORIENTAL CHICKEN-NOODLE SOUP

Give this soup even more of an Oriental flare by cutting four wonton skins into thin strips instead of using the fine egg noodles.

2   14½-ounce cans chicken broth
1   cup water
1   medium sweet red pepper, cut into
        ¾-inch pieces (1 cup)
½   cup chopped carrot
½   cup fine egg noodles
⅓   cup thinly sliced green onion
1   tablespoon soy sauce
1   teaspoon grated gingerroot
⅛   teaspoon crushed red pepper
1   cup chopped cooked chicken *or* turkey
1   cup fresh pea pods, halved crosswise,
        or ½ of a 6-ounce package frozen
        pea pods, thawed and halved
        crosswise

In a large saucepan or Dutch oven combine chicken broth, water, sweet red pepper, carrot, egg noodles, green onion, soy sauce, gingerroot, and crushed red pepper. Bring to boiling. Reduce heat and simmer, covered, for 4 to 6 minutes or till vegetables are crisp-tender and noodles are tender.

Stir in chicken or turkey and pea pods. Simmer, uncovered, for 1 to 2 minutes more or till pea pods are crisp-tender. Makes 3 to 4 servings.

Nutrition information per serving: 217 calories, 24 g protein, 15 g carbohydrate, 6 g fat (2 g saturated), 53 mg cholesterol, 1,343 mg sodium, 616 mg potassium.

MEXICAN CHICKEN-TORTILLA SOUP

This soup features cilantro, a fresh herb that looks like a flattened parsley leaf, but has a pungent, almost musty odor and taste that gives a distinctive flavor to Mexican dishes.

3½ cups chicken broth
2 whole small chicken breasts
    (about 1¼ pounds total)
½ cup chopped onion
½ teaspoon ground cumin
1 clove garlic, minced
1 tablespoon cooking oil
1 16-ounce can tomatoes, cut up
1 8-ounce can tomato sauce
1 4-ounce can whole green chili
    peppers, rinsed, seeded, and cut
    into thin bite-size strips
¼ cup snipped fresh cilantro *or* parsley
1 tablespoon snipped fresh oregano *or* 1
    teaspoon dried oregano, crushed
6 5½-inch corn tortillas
    Cooking oil
1 cup shredded cheddar *or* Monterey
    Jack cheese (4 ounces)

Place chicken broth in a large saucepan or Dutch oven; add chicken breasts. Bring to boiling. Reduce heat and simmer, covered, about 15 minutes or till chicken is tender and no longer pink. Remove chicken from broth. Let stand till cool enough to handle. Skin, bone, and finely shred chicken; set chicken aside. Discard skin and bones. Strain broth through a large sieve or colander lined with 2 layers of *100% cotton* cheesecloth. Skim fat from broth and set broth aside.

In the same saucepan cook onion, cumin, and garlic in the 1 tablespoon hot oil till onion is tender but not brown. Stir in strained broth, *undrained* tomatoes, tomato sauce, chili peppers, cilantro or parsley, and oregano. Bring to boiling. Reduce heat and simmer, covered, for 20 minutes. Stir in shredded chicken; heat through.

Meanwhile, cut tortillas in half, then cut crosswise into ½-inch-wide strips. In a heavy medium skillet heat ¼ inch oil. Fry strips in hot oil, about half at a time, about 1 minute or till crisp and light brown. Remove with a slotted spoon; drain on paper towels.

Divide fried tortilla strips among four soup bowls. Ladle soup over tortilla strips. Sprinkle each serving with shredded cheese. Serve immediately. Makes 4 servings.

Nutrition information per serving: 496 calories, 38 g protein, 33 g carbohydrate, 24 g fat (8 g saturated), 85 mg cholesterol, 1,658 mg sodium, 1,015 mg potassium.

EASY MULLIGATAWNY SOUP

This is an easy version of the golden-colored, curry-flavored soup from India.

2½ cups chicken broth
 1 cup water
 1 cup chopped apple
 1 cup chopped carrot
 1 7½-ounce can tomatoes, cut up
 ½ cup chopped celery
 ⅓ cup long grain rice
 ¼ cup chopped onion
 ¼ cup raisins
 1 tablespoon snipped fresh cilantro *or*
      parsley
 1 to 1½ teaspoons curry powder
 1 teaspoon lemon juice
 ¼ teaspoon coarsely ground pepper
 ⅛ teaspoon ground mace *or* nutmeg
1½ cups chopped cooked chicken

In a large saucepan combine broth, water, apple, carrot, *undrained* tomatoes, celery, uncooked rice, onion, raisins, cilantro or parsley, curry powder, lemon juice, pepper, and mace or nutmeg. Bring to boiling. Reduce heat and simmer, covered, about 20 minutes, or till rice is tender. Stir in chicken and heat through. Makes 4 servings.

Nutrition information per serving: 259 calories, 22 g protein, 30 g carbohydrate, 6 g fat (1 g saturated), 51 mg cholesterol, 665 mg sodium, 644 mg potassium.

QUICK-TO-FIX TURKEY AND RICE SOUP

Turn your leftover Thanksgiving turkey into a meal your family will love.

4 cups chicken broth
1 cup water
1 teaspoon snipped fresh rosemary *or* ¼
   teaspoon dried rosemary, crushed
¼ teaspoon pepper
1 10-ounce package frozen mixed
   vegetables (2 cups)
1 cup quick-cooking rice
2 cups chopped cooked turkey *or*
   chicken
1 16-ounce can tomatoes, cut up

In a large saucepan or Dutch oven combine chicken broth, water, rosemary, and pepper. Bring to boiling.

Stir in mixed vegetables and rice. Return to boiling. Reduce heat and simmer, covered, for 10 to 15 minutes or till vegetables and rice are tender. Stir in turkey or chicken and *undrained* tomatoes; heat through. Makes 6 servings.

Nutrition information per serving: 209 calories, 20 g protein, 24 g carbohydrate, 4 g fat (1 g saturated), 36 mg cholesterol, 699 mg sodium, 540 mg potassium.

CAJUN SEAFOOD GUMBO

Add a bit of the bayou—okra, seafood, and tongue-tingling spices—to your menu with this Cajun specialty.

12 ounces fresh *or* frozen peeled and
    deveined shrimp
6 ounces fresh *or* frozen crabmeat
⅓ cup all-purpose flour
¼ cup cooking oil
½ cup chopped onion
½ cup chopped sweet red pepper
½ cup chopped green pepper
4 cloves garlic, minced
¼ teaspoon salt
¼ teaspoon black pepper
¼ teaspoon ground red pepper
3 cups chicken broth, heated
1 16-ounce can tomatoes, cut up
1½ cups sliced okra *or* one 10-ounce
    package frozen cut okra
2 bay leaves
½ pint shucked oysters, drained
3 cups hot cooked rice

Thaw shrimp and crab, if frozen. For roux, in a large heavy saucepan or Dutch oven combine flour and oil till smooth. Cook over medium-high heat for 5 minutes, stirring constantly. Reduce heat to medium. Cook and stir about 10 minutes more or till roux is light reddish brown.

Stir in onion, sweet red pepper, green pepper, garlic, salt, black pepper, and ground red pepper. Cook over medium heat for 3 to 5 minutes or till vegetables are just crisp-tender, stirring often.

Gradually stir in hot chicken broth. Stir in *undrained* tomatoes, okra, and bay leaves. Bring to boiling. Reduce heat and simmer, covered, for 30 minutes.

Stir in shrimp, crabmeat, and oysters. Simmer, covered, about 5 minutes more or till shrimp turn pink and oysters curl around the edges. Discard bay leaves. Serve in bowls with rice. Makes 6 servings.

Nutrition information per serving: 394 calories, 25 g protein, 45 g carbohydrate, 12 g fat (2 g saturated), 123 mg cholesterol, 1,058 mg sodium, 757 mg potassium.

OYSTER SOUP

Oyster soup is mildly seasoned so the delicate fish flavor comes through. If you like, float a small pat of margarine or butter atop each serving.

¼ cup finely chopped onion *or* sliced leek
2 teaspoons margarine *or* butter
1 pint shucked oysters
½ teaspoon salt
2 cups milk
1 cup half-and-half *or* light cream
1 tablespoon snipped fresh parsley
1 tablespoon chopped pimiento (optional)
¼ teaspoon white pepper

In a medium saucepan cook onion or leek in margarine or butter till tender but not brown. Add the *undrained* oysters and salt. Cook over medium heat about 5 minutes or till oysters curl around the edges, stirring occasionally.

Stir in milk, half-and-half or light cream, parsley, pimiento (if desired), and pepper. Heat through. Makes 4 servings.

Nutrition information per serving: 239 calories, 14 g protein, 14 g carbohydrate, 14 g fat (7 g saturated), 93 mg cholesterol, 502 mg sodium, 549 mg potassium.

TEX-MEX SEAFOOD GAZPACHO

This snappy soup tastes best when it's been thoroughly chilled and then served in chilled bowls.

8 ounces fresh *or* frozen peeled and
  deveined small shrimp
8 ounces fresh *or* frozen bay scallops
4 cups water
¼ teaspoon salt
4 cups chopped, peeled tomatoes
2 cups chopped, seeded cucumber
1 cup chopped green pepper
2 5½-ounce cans (1⅓ cups total) hot-
  style vegetable juice cocktail
2 tablespoons sliced green onion
1 tablespoon chopped jalapeño pepper
1 tablespoon snipped fresh cilantro *or*
  parsley
1 tablespoon lemon juice *or* lime juice
¼ teaspoon salt
1 clove garlic, halved
  Snipped fresh cilantro *or* parsley
  (optional)

Thaw shrimp and scallops, if frozen. In a large saucepan bring water and ¼ teaspoon salt to boiling. Add shrimp and scallops. Simmer, uncovered, for 1 to 3 minutes or till shrimp turn pink and scallops are opaque, stirring occasionally. Drain shrimp and scallops; cover and chill.

Meanwhile, set aside 1 cup of the chopped tomato, 1 cup of the chopped cucumber, and ½ cup of the chopped green pepper. In a large mixing bowl combine remaining chopped tomato, remaining chopped cucumber, remaining green pepper, the vegetable juice cocktail, green onion, jalapeño pepper, 1 tablespoon cilantro or parsley, lemon juice or lime juice, ¼ teaspoon salt, and garlic.

In a blender container or food processor bowl cover and blend or process mixture, half at a time, till smooth. Return to the large mixing bowl. Stir in reserved chopped tomato, cucumber, and green pepper. Cover and chill for 2 to 24 hours.

Just before serving, stir in shrimp and scallops. If desired, garnish each serving with additional cilantro or parsley. Makes 4 servings.

Nutrition information per serving: 164 calories, 19 g protein, 19 g carbohydrate, 2 g fat (0 g saturated), 104 mg cholesterol, 754 mg sodium, 1,088 mg potassium.

CHUNKY VEGETABLE-COD SOUP

This fish soup will win your family's approval. . .hook, line, and sinker!

1 pound fresh *or* frozen skinless cod
   fillets *or* steaks
½ cup chopped sweet red pepper
¼ cup chopped onion
1 tablespoon margarine *or* butter
3½ cups vegetable broth *or* chicken broth
1 cup frozen cut green beans
1 cup coarsely chopped cabbage
½ cup sliced carrot
1 teaspoon snipped fresh basil *or* ¼
   teaspoon dried basil, crushed
1 teaspoon snipped fresh thyme *or* ¼
   teaspoon dried thyme, crushed
½ teaspoon snipped fresh rosemary *or* ⅛
   teaspoon dried rosemary, crushed
¼ teaspoon pepper
   Lemon wedges (optional)

Thaw cod, if frozen; cut into 1-inch pieces. In a large saucepan or Dutch oven cook sweet red pepper and onion in margarine or butter till tender. Stir in vegetable broth or chicken broth, green beans, cabbage, carrot, basil, thyme, rosemary, and pepper. Bring to boiling. Reduce heat and simmer, covered, for 8 to 10 minutes or till vegetables are nearly tender.

Add fish to saucepan. Return to boiling. Reduce heat and simmer, covered, about 5 minutes or till fish flakes easily with a fork, stirring once. If desired, serve with lemon wedges. Makes 4 servings.

Nutrition information per serving: 140 calories, 20 g protein, 9 g carbohydrate, 5 g fat (1 g saturated), 45 mg cholesterol, 922 mg sodium, 365 mg potassium.

SOUTHWESTERN BEAN SOUP WITH CORNMEAL DUMPLINGS

Healthful and hearty, this meatless bean and vegetable soup will satisfy any hungry gang.

3 cups water
1 15½-ounce can red kidney beans, rinsed and drained
1 15-ounce can black beans, pinto beans, *or* great northern beans, rinsed and drained
1 14½-ounce can Mexican-style stewed tomatoes
1 10-ounce package frozen whole kernel corn
1 cup sliced carrot
1 cup chopped onion
1 4-ounce can diced green chili peppers
2 tablespoons instant beef *or* chicken bouillon granules
1 to 2 teaspoons chili powder
2 cloves garlic, minced
⅓ cup all-purpose flour
¼ cup yellow cornmeal
1 teaspoon baking powder
Dash salt
Dash pepper
1 beaten egg white
2 tablespoons milk
1 tablespoon cooking oil

In a 4-quart Dutch oven combine water, kidney beans, black beans, *undrained* tomatoes, corn, carrot, onion, *undrained* chili peppers, bouillon granules, chili powder, and garlic. Bring to boiling. Reduce heat and simmer, covered, for 10 minutes.

Meanwhile, for dumplings, in a medium mixing bowl stir together flour, cornmeal, baking powder, salt, and pepper. In a small mixing bowl combine egg white, milk, and oil. Add to flour mixture; stir with a fork just till combined. Drop dumpling mixture into 6 mounds atop the bubbling soup. Cover and simmer for 12 to 15 minutes or till a toothpick comes out clean. (Do not lift lid while dumplings are cooking.) Makes 6 servings.

Crockery cooker directions: In a 3½- or 4-quart crockery cooker combine water, beans, *undrained* tomatoes, corn, carrot, onion, *undrained* chili peppers, bouillon granules, chili powder, and garlic. Cover and cook on low-heat setting for 10 to 12 hours. Prepare dumplings and drop onto soup as directed above. Cover and cook for 30 minutes more. (Do not lift lid while dumplings are cooking.)

Nutrition information per serving: 270 calories, 15 g protein, 54 g carbohydrate, 3 g fat (1 g saturated), 1 mg cholesterol, 1,593 mg sodium, 696 mg potassium.

SHERRIED BLACK BEAN SOUP

If you can't find canned black beans in your supermarket, use canned kidney beans instead.

½ cup thinly sliced carrot
⅓ cup chopped onion
4 cloves garlic, minced
1 tablespoon cooking oil
2 teaspoons ground cumin
4 cups water
2 15-ounce cans black beans, rinsed and
     drained
1 cup cubed fully cooked ham
¼ cup dry sherry *or* water
1 teaspoon instant beef *or* chicken
     bouillon granules
1 tablespoon snipped fresh oregano *or*
     1 teaspoon dried oregano, crushed
⅛ teaspoon ground red pepper
2 bay leaves
¼ cup dairy sour cream
¼ cup frozen peas, thawed

In a large saucepan cook carrots, onion, and garlic in hot oil over medium-low heat for 3 minutes. Stir in cumin and cook till carrots are tender. Stir in water, beans, ham, sherry or water, bouillon granules, oregano, ground red pepper, and bay leaves. Bring to boiling. Reduce heat and simmer, uncovered, for 25 minutes. Remove and discard bay leaves.

To serve, ladle into bowls and top with sour cream and a few peas. Makes 4 servings.

Nutrition information per serving: 294 calories, 23 g protein, 37 g carbohydrate, 9 g fat (3 g saturated), 17 mg cholesterol, 1,174 mg sodium, 696 mg potassium.

POTATO-BEAN SOUP

To save about 150 mg of sodium per serving, use lower-sodium chicken broth.

2   medium carrots, shredded (1 cup)
½   cup sliced celery
1   clove garlic, minced
1   tablespoon margarine *or* butter
4   cups chicken broth
3   cups cubed, peeled potatoes
2   tablespoons snipped fresh dill *or*
      2 teaspoons dried dillweed
1   15-ounce can cannellini beans *or* great
      northern beans, rinsed and drained
½   cup dairy sour cream *or* plain nonfat
      yogurt
1   tablespoon all-purpose flour
⅛   teaspoon pepper
      Dash salt (optional)

In a large saucepan cook and stir carrots, celery, and garlic in hot margarine or butter over medium heat for 4 minutes or till tender. Carefully stir in chicken broth, potatoes, and dill. Bring to boiling. Reduce heat and simmer, covered, for 20 to 25 minutes or till potatoes are tender. With the back of a spoon, lightly mash about half of the potatoes in the broth. Stir the beans into the potato mixture.

In a small mixing bowl stir together the sour cream or yogurt, flour, pepper, and, if desired, salt; stir into potato mixture. Cook and stir till thickened and bubbly. Cook and stir for 1 minute more. Makes 4 to 6 servings.

Nutrition information per serving: 296 calories, 14 g protein, 42 g carbohydrate, 11 g fat (5 g saturated), 13 mg cholesterol, 1,031 mg sodium, 868 mg potassium.

MINESTRONE

The countless versions of this classic Italian vegetable soup all have one thing in common—they're full of beans, pasta, and vegetables.

2   14½-ounce cans chicken broth *or* beef broth
1   16-ounce can tomatoes, cut up
1   cup chopped onion
1   cup shredded cabbage
¾   cup tomato juice
½   cup chopped carrot
½   cup sliced celery
1   tablespoon snipped fresh basil *or* 1 teaspoon dried basil, crushed
¼   teaspoon garlic powder
1   15-ounce can cannellini beans *or* great northern beans, rinsed and drained
1   medium zucchini, sliced ¼ inch thick (1 cup)
½   of a 9-ounce package frozen Italian-style green beans
2   ounces spaghetti *or* linguine, broken (about ½ cup)
2   tablespoons shaved *or* finely shredded Parmesan cheese

In a Dutch oven combine chicken broth or beef broth, *undrained* tomatoes, onion, cabbage, tomato juice, carrot, celery, basil, and garlic powder. Bring to boiling. Reduce heat and simmer, covered, for 20 minutes.

Stir in cannellini beans or great northern beans, zucchini, green beans, and spaghetti or linguine. Return to boiling. Reduce heat and simmer, covered, for 10 to 15 minutes or till vegetables and pasta are tender. Top each serving with Parmesan cheese. Makes 4 servings.

Nutrition information per serving: 243 calories, 17 g protein, 44 g carbohydrate, 3 g fat (1 g saturated), 2 mg cholesterol, 1,315 mg sodium, 1,068 mg potassium.

LENTIL SOUP

This robust soup is a good choice when you're short on time—it cooks in just about 35 minutes.

1 cup dry lentils
5 cups water
1 cup chopped green pepper
1 cup sliced carrot
½ cup chopped onion
2 teaspoons instant chicken bouillon granules
2 teaspoons snipped fresh sage *or* ½ teaspoon dried sage, crushed
⅛ teaspoon ground red pepper
2 cloves garlic, minced
½ pound fully cooked smoked sausage links, sliced diagonally
Snipped fresh parsley (optional)

Rinse and drain lentils. In a large saucepan or Dutch oven combine lentils, water, green pepper, carrot, onion, bouillon granules, sage, ground red pepper, and garlic. Bring to boiling. Reduce heat and simmer, covered, about 30 minutes or till vegetables and lentils are tender. Stir in sausage and heat through. If desired, garnish each serving with parsley. Makes 4 servings.

Nutrition information per serving: 285 calories, 24 g protein, 38 g carbohydrate, 5 g fat (1 g saturated), 36 mg cholesterol, 945 mg sodium, 789 mg potassium.

CHEESE SOUP WITH JALAPEÑO PESTO

This rich and creamy cheese soup gets a flavor punch from the fresh-tasting, hot pepper pesto.

3   cups chicken broth
1½ cups shredded carrot
1   cup chopped green onion
¼   cup tomato paste
2½ cups milk
¼   cup all-purpose flour
1   teaspoon dry mustard
¼   teaspoon pepper
2   3-ounce packages cream cheese, cut into cubes and softened
3   cups shredded sharp cheddar *or* American cheese (12 ounces)
   Jalapeño Pesto

In a large saucepan stir together chicken broth, carrot, green onion, and tomato paste. Bring to boiling. Reduce heat and simmer, covered, for 2 minutes. Combine milk, flour, mustard, and pepper; stir into chicken broth mixture. Cook and stir over medium heat till thickened and bubbly. Cook and stir for 1 minute more.

In a mixing bowl stir about 1 cup of the hot milk mixture into cream cheese; stir till smooth. Stir cream cheese mixture back into remaining milk mixture in saucepan. Stir cheddar or American cheese into mixture in saucepan till melted.

Spoon a scant 1 tablespoon Jalapeño Pesto atop each serving. Makes 4 or 5 servings.

Jalapeño Pesto: In a blender container or food processor bowl combine ¼ cup firmly packed fresh *cilantro leaves;* ¼ cup firmly packed *parsley sprigs* with stems removed; 3 tablespoons grated *Parmesan cheese;* 2 tablespoons *olive oil or cooking oil;* ¼ teaspoon finely shredded *lime peel;* 1 teaspoon *lime juice;* 2 *jalapeño peppers,* cut up; and 1 clove garlic, minced. Cover and blend or process till a paste forms. Cover and chill up to 2 days. Makes about ⅓ cup.

Nutrition information per serving: 831 calories, 39 g protein, 34 g carbohydrate, 61 g fat (33 g saturated), 152 mg cholesterol, 1,523 mg sodium, 906 mg potassium.

CHILI WITH CHEESY CORNMEAL DUMPLINGS

Fluffy dumplings top this mildly seasoned chili—perfect for a family-style dinner on a wintery day.

¾ **pound ground beef**
1 **cup chopped onion**
½ **cup chopped green pepper**
2 **cloves garlic, minced**
1 **16-ounce can tomatoes, cut up**
1 **15-ounce can dark red kidney beans,**
    rinsed and drained
1 **8-ounce can tomato sauce**
½ **cup water**
1 **tablespoon chili powder**
½ **teaspoon ground cumin**
¼ **teaspoon salt**
¼ **teaspoon pepper**
    Cheesy Cornmeal Dumplings

In a large saucepan or Dutch oven cook ground beef, onion, green pepper, and garlic till meat is brown and onion is tender. Drain fat from pan. Stir in *undrained* tomatoes, kidney beans, tomato sauce, water, chili powder, cumin, salt, and pepper. Bring to boiling. Reduce heat and simmer, uncovered, for 5 minutes.

Drop Cheesy Cornmeal Dumplings by tablespoonfuls onto simmering chili. Simmer, covered, about 20 minutes more or till a toothpick inserted into dumplings comes out clean. Makes 4 servings.

Cheesy Cornmeal Dumplings: In a medium mixing bowl stir together ½ cup *all-purpose flour,* ½ cup shredded *cheddar cheese* (2 ounces), ⅓ cup *yellow cornmeal,* 1 teaspoon *baking powder,* and dash *pepper.* Combine 1 beaten *egg,* 2 tablespoons *milk,* and 2 tablespoons *cooking oil;* add to flour mixture. Stir with a fork just till combined.

Nutrition information per serving: 528 calories, 35 g protein, 55 g carbohydrate, 22 g fat (8 g saturated), 122 mg cholesterol, 1,108 mg sodium, 1,036 mg potassium.

WHITE CHILI WITH SALSA VERDE

This wintertime dish looks like navy bean soup, but tastes like a mild-flavored chili. It's topped with a spicy Mexican salsa that's made with tomatillos.

¾ **pound ground raw turkey**
½ **cup chopped onion**
1 **clove garlic, minced**
3 **cups water**
1 **15-ounce can great northern *or* cannellini beans, rinsed and drained**
1 **4-ounce can diced green chili peppers**
2 **teaspoons instant chicken bouillon granules**
1 **teaspoon ground cumin**
¼ **teaspoon pepper**
¼ **cup water**
2 **tablespoons all-purpose flour**
1 **cup shredded Monterey Jack cheese (4 ounces)**
   Salsa Verde

In a large saucepan or Dutch oven cook ground turkey, onion, and garlic till turkey is no longer pink and onion is tender. Drain fat from pan, if necessary.

Stir in the 3 cups water, beans, *undrained* chili peppers, chicken bouillon granules, cumin, and pepper. Bring to boiling. Reduce heat and simmer, covered, for 30 minutes.

In a small bowl stir together the ¼ cup water and the flour. Add flour mixture to the chili mixture. Cook and stir till thickened and bubbly. Cook and stir for 1 minute more. Top each serving with some of the shredded cheese and the Salsa Verde. Makes 4 servings.

Salsa Verde: In a medium mixing bowl stir together 5 or 6 fresh *tomatillos* (6 to 8 ounces), husks removed, and finely chopped, or one 13-ounce can tomatillos, drained, rinsed, and finely chopped; 2 tablespoons finely chopped *onion; 2 serrano or jalapeño peppers,* seeded and finely chopped; 1 tablespoon snipped fresh *cilantro or parsley;* 1 teaspoon finely shredded *lime peel;* and ½ teaspoon *sugar.* Cover and chill up to 2 days or freeze; thaw before using.

Nutrition information per serving: 319 calories, 26 g protein, 24 g carbohydrate, 16 g fat (7 g saturated), 57 mg cholesterol, 927 mg sodium, 519 mg potassium.

VEGETARIAN CHILI

In this spicy, meatless chili, the protein comes from beans and cheese instead of meat.

3   cloves garlic, minced
1   tablespoon cooking oil
2   14½-ounce cans chili-style chunky
      tomatoes
1   12-ounce can beer
1   cup water
1   8-ounce can tomato sauce
1   tablespoon chili powder
1   tablespoon Dijon-style mustard
1   tablespoon snipped fresh oregano *or*
      1 teaspoon dried oregano, crushed
1   teaspoon ground cumin
½   teaspoon pepper
    Several dashes bottled hot pepper
      sauce
1   15-ounce can pinto beans, rinsed and
      drained
1   15-ounce can cannellini beans, rinsed
      and drained
1   15-ounce can red kidney beans, rinsed
      and drained
1½ cups fresh *or* frozen whole kernel corn
1½ cups chopped zucchini *or* yellow
      summer squash
¾   cup shredded cheddar *or* Monterey
      Jack cheese (6 ounces)

In a Dutch oven cook garlic in hot oil for 30 seconds. Stir in the *undrained* tomatoes, beer, water, tomato sauce, chili powder, mustard, oregano, cumin, pepper, and hot pepper sauce. Stir in the pinto beans, cannellini beans, and red kidney beans. Bring mixture to boiling. Reduce heat and simmer, covered, for 10 minutes.

Stir in the corn and zucchini or yellow summer squash. Simmer, covered, about 10 minutes or till vegetables are tender. Spoon into serving bowls. Top each serving with *2 tablespoons* shredded cheese. Makes 6 servings.

Nutrition information per serving: 320 calories, 21 g protein, 57 g carbohydrate, 8 g fat (3 g saturated), 15 mg cholesterol, 1,573 mg sodium, 1,005 mg potassium.

TEXAS-STYLE BOWLS OF RED

Texans have a high tolerance for hot and spicy foods, so if you're not from the Lone Star state, taste this extra-hot, authentic chili at your own risk!

20 small dried hot chili peppers *or*
  2 tablespoons crushed red pepper
2 dried ancho peppers *or* 2 tablespoons
  chili powder
¾ pound beef round steak, cut into
  ½-inch cubes
¾ pound boneless pork, cut into
  ½-inch cubes
2 tablespoons cooking oil
1 cup chopped onion
3 cloves garlic, minced
1 tablespoon ground cumin
½ teaspoon paprika
¼ teaspoon ground black pepper
1 14½-ounce can beef broth
1 12-ounce can beer
3 cups hot cooked pinto beans *and/or*
  hot cooked rice
  Sliced jalapeño peppers (optional)

Crush hot chili peppers, if using. Remove stems and seeds from ancho peppers, if using; cut into 1-inch pieces. Put hot peppers and ancho peppers into a blender container or food processor bowl. Cover and blend or process till ground. Let pepper dust settle before opening blender or food processor. (If using crushed red pepper and chili powder, stir them together.) Set aside.

In a large saucepan or Dutch oven cook half of the meat in hot oil till brown. Remove meat and set aside. Add remaining meat, onion, garlic, cumin, paprika, ground black pepper, and ground chili pepper mixture (or the crushed red pepper and chili powder mixture, if using). Cook till meat is brown. Return all meat to saucepan. Stir in beef broth and beer. Bring to boiling. Reduce heat and simmer, covered, for 45 minutes. Uncover and simmer about 30 minutes more or till meat is tender and sauce is desired consistency, stirring occasionally. Serve with hot cooked pinto beans or rice. Garnish with sliced jalapeño peppers, if desired. Makes 6 servings.

Nutrition information per serving: 340 calories, 26 g protein, 34 g carbohydrate, 10 g fat (2 g saturated), 44 mg cholesterol, 445 mg sodium, 875 mg potassium.

OLD-FASHIONED BEEF STEW

Take the hassle out of dinner tonight by letting this scrumptious stew simmer in your crockery cooker all day.

2	tablespoons all-purpose flour
1	pound beef *or* pork stew meat, cut into ¾-inch cubes
2	tablespoons cooking oil
3½	cups vegetable juice cocktail
1	medium onion, cut into thin wedges
2	teaspoons instant beef bouillon granules
2	teaspoons Worcestershire sauce
1½	teaspoons snipped fresh marjoram *or* ½ teaspoon dried marjoram, crushed
1½	teaspoons snipped fresh oregano *or* ½ teaspoon dried oregano, crushed
¼	teaspoon pepper
1	bay leaf
2½	cups cubed potatoes
1	cup frozen cut green beans
1	cup frozen whole kernel corn
1	cup sliced carrot

Place flour in a plastic bag. Add meat cubes, a few at a time, shaking to coat. In a large saucepan or Dutch oven brown meat, *half* at a time, in hot oil. Drain fat from pan. Return meat to saucepan. Stir in vegetable juice cocktail, onion, bouillon granules, Worcestershire sauce, marjoram, oregano, pepper, and bay leaf. Bring to boiling. Reduce heat and simmer, covered, for 1 to 1¼ hours for beef (about 30 minutes for pork) or till meat is nearly tender.

Stir in potatoes, green beans, corn, and carrot. Bring to boiling. Reduce heat and simmer, covered, about 30 minutes more or till meat and vegetables are tender. Discard bay leaf. Makes 4 servings.

Crockery-cooker directions: Prepare and brown meat as above. In the bottom of a 3½- or 4-quart electric crockery cooker layer meat, onion, potatoes, green beans, corn, and carrot. Decrease vegetable juice cocktail to 2½ cups. Combine vegetable juice cocktail, bouillon granules, Worcestershire sauce, marjoram, oregano, pepper, and bay leaf. Pour over meat and vegetables in crockery cooker. Cover and cook on low-heat setting for 10 to 12 hours or till meat and vegetables are tender.

Nutrition information per serving: 458 calories, 30 g protein, 48 g carbohydrate, 16 g fat (6 g saturated), 84 mg cholesterol, 1,261 mg sodium, 1,236 mg potassium.

GINGERED BEEF-VEGETABLE STEW

Sherry, soy sauce, and gingerroot give this chunky stew an oriental twist.

1	pound beef *or* pork stew meat, cut into ¾-inch cubes
2	tablespoons cooking oil
2½	cups water
1	medium onion, cut into thin wedges
⅓	cup dry sherry
3	tablespoons soy sauce
1½	teaspoons grated gingerroot
½	teaspoon sugar
1½	cups broccoli flowerets
1	cup thinly sliced carrots
1	large sweet red *or* green pepper, cut into ¾-inch pieces (1 cup)
1	8-ounce can sliced water chestnuts, drained
¼	cup water
3	tablespoons cornstarch
	Soy sauce (optional)

In a large saucepan or Dutch oven brown beef or pork, *half* at a time, in hot oil. Drain fat from pan. Return beef or pork to saucepan. Stir in the 2½ cups water, onion, dry sherry, 3 tablespoons soy sauce, gingerroot, and sugar. Bring to boiling. Reduce heat and simmer, covered, for 1 to 1¼ hours for beef (about 30 minutes for pork) or till meat is nearly tender.

Stir in broccoli, carrots, sweet red or green pepper, and water chestnuts. Cover and simmer about 10 minutes more or till meat and vegetables are tender.

Stir together the ¼ cup water and the cornstarch; stir into soup. Cook and stir till thickened and bubbly. Cook and stir for 2 minutes more. If desired, serve with additional soy sauce. Makes 4 servings.

Nutrition information per serving: 397 calories, 28 g protein, 23 g carbohydrate, 19 g fat (6 g saturated), 84 mg cholesterol, 876 mg sodium, 608 mg potassium.

OVEN-BAKED PORK STEW

Mouth-watering pork, a variety of vegetables, and a well-flavored gravy bake into a stew that is sure to get rave reviews.

1½ pounds pork *or* beef stew meat,
      cut into ¾-inch cubes
1   tablespoon cooking oil
3   cups beef broth
½   pound pearl onions *or* 2 cups frozen
      whole small onions
1   tablespoon snipped fresh oregano *or*
      1 teaspoon dried oregano, crushed
1½ teaspoons snipped fresh marjoram *or*
      ½ teaspoon dried marjoram,
      crushed
1   teaspoon lemon-pepper seasoning
¼   teaspoon garlic powder
½   cup cold water
¼   cup all-purpose flour
4   medium potatoes, cut into 1-inch
      pieces (4 cups)
4   medium carrots, cut into 1-inch
      pieces (1½ cups)
1   cup fresh *or* frozen cut green beans

In a Dutch oven brown meat, *half* at a time, in hot oil. Drain fat from pan. Return all meat to pan. Stir in beef broth, onions, oregano, marjoram, lemon-pepper seasoning, and garlic powder. Bring to boiling. Remove from heat. Cover tightly and bake in a 325° oven for 45 minutes.

Combine water and flour; stir into stew. Stir in potatoes, carrots, and green beans. Bake, covered, for 1¼ hours more or till meat and vegetables are tender and mixture is thickened. Makes 6 servings.

Nutrition information per serving: 361 calories, 25 g protein, 36 g carbohydrate, 13 g fat (4 g saturated), 74 mg cholesterol, 671 mg sodium, 942 mg potassium.

PORK AND MUSHROOM STEW

This hearty soup is sure to satisfy the biggest of appetites.

1   pound pork stew meat, cut into
      1-inch cubes
2   tablespoons margarine *or* butter
1   10½-ounce can condensed chicken
      broth
¼   cup dry white wine
3   tablespoons snipped fresh parsley
¾   teaspoon snipped fresh thyme *or*
      ¼ teaspoon dried thyme, crushed
¼   teaspoon garlic powder
⅛   teaspoon pepper
1   bay leaf
2   cups frozen whole small onions
1   10-ounce package frozen tiny whole
      carrots
1   4-ounce can whole mushrooms,
      drained
¾   cup cold water
¼   cup all-purpose flour
1   tablespoon lemon juice

In a large saucepan brown pork, *half* at a time, in margarine or butter. Return all meat to pan. Stir in the chicken broth, wine, parsley, thyme, garlic powder, pepper, and bay leaf. Bring to boiling. Reduce heat and simmer, covered, for 40 minutes.

Add the frozen onions, frozen carrots, and mushrooms. Return to boiling. Reduce heat and simmer, covered, about 15 minutes more or till vegetables are tender. Remove bay leaf.

Combine cold water and flour; add to stew with lemon juice. Cook and stir till thickened and bubbly. Cook and stir for 1 minute more. Makes 4 servings.

Nutrition information per serving: 361 calories, 26 g protein, 20 g carbohydrate, 18 g fat (5 g saturated), 74 mg cholesterol, 800 mg sodium, 746 mg potassium.

SPICED APRICOT LAMB STEW

This low-calorie stew is seasoned with turmeric, a bright, yellow-orange spice that's a major ingredient in curry powder.

1½ pounds lamb stew meat, cut into
     1-inch cubes
½   cup chopped onion
¼   cup water
3   tablespoons honey
1   tablespoon lemon juice
3   inches stick cinnamon
1   teaspoon ground turmeric
2   cloves garlic, minced
¼   teaspoon salt
½   of a 6-ounce package dried apricots,
     snipped
1   tablespoon water
1   teaspoon cornstarch
3   cups hot cooked orzo *or* rice
    Parsley (optional)

In a large saucepan combine the lamb, onion, the ¼ cup water, honey, lemon juice, cinnamon, turmeric, garlic, and salt. Bring to boiling. Reduce heat and simmer, covered, for 40 to 55 minutes or till lamb is nearly tender. Stir in the apricots. Simmer, covered, about 5 minutes more or till lamb is tender.

Stir together the 1 tablespoon water and the cornstarch; stir into lamb mixture. Cook and stir till thickened and bubbly. Cook and stir for 2 minutes more. Remove cinnamon stick. Serve stew with orzo or rice. Garnish with parsely, if desired. Makes 6 servings.

Nutrition information per serving: 296 calories, 23 g protein, 39 g carbohydrate, 6 g fat (2 g saturated), 57 mg cholesterol, 136 mg sodium, 508 mg potassium.

MIDEASTERN LAMB STEW WITH COUSCOUS

Couscous (KOOS koos) is a semolina pasta that's very tiny. Prepare it according to package directions.

1 pound lamb stew meat, cut into
¾-inch cubes
2 tablespoons olive oil *or* cooking oil
2½ cups beef broth
1 8-ounce can tomato sauce
1 cup chopped onion
1 tablespoon lemon juice
1 clove garlic, minced
¾ teaspoon ground cumin
½ teaspoon ground turmeric
¼ teaspoon salt
¼ teaspoon pepper
1 small eggplant (about 1 pound)
peeled and cut into ¾-inch cubes
(4 cups)
1 cup chopped sweet red pepper
¼ cup raisins
⅓ cup cold water
3 tablespoons all-purpose flour
3 cups hot cooked couscous

In a Dutch oven brown meat in hot olive oil or cooking oil. Drain fat from pan. Stir in beef broth, tomato sauce, onion, lemon juice, garlic, cumin, turmeric, salt, and pepper. Bring to boiling. Reduce heat and simmer, covered, for 30 minutes. Stir in eggplant, sweet red pepper, and raisins. Bring to boiling. Reduce heat and simmer, covered, about 30 minutes more or till meat and vegetables are tender. If necessary, skim fat from stew.

Combine cold water and flour. Stir flour mixture into stew. Cook and stir till thickened and bubbly. Cook and stir for 1 minute more. Serve stew with hot cooked couscous. Makes 4 servings.

Nutrition information per serving: 452 calories, 28 g protein, 57 g carbohydrate, 13 g fat (3 g saturated), 57 mg cholesterol, 1,049 mg sodium, 930 mg potassium.

LAMB AND WINTER VEGETABLE STEW

If lamb stew meat isn't available in your supermarket, buy a lamb shoulder roast, trim off the fat, and cut it into ¾-inch cubes.

1   **pound lamb stew meat, cut into ¾-inch cubes**
2   **tablespoons cooking oil**
2   **cups beef broth**
1   **cup dry red wine *or* beef broth**
2   **cloves garlic, minced**
1   **tablespoon snipped fresh thyme *or* 1 teaspoon dried thyme, crushed**
¼   **teaspoon salt**
¼   **teaspoon pepper**
1   **bay leaf**
2   **cups cubed, peeled butternut squash**
1   **cup parsnips cut into ½-inch slices**
1   **cup chopped, peeled sweet potatoes**
1   **cup sliced celery**
1   **medium onion, cut into thin wedges**
½   **cup dairy sour cream**
3   **tablespoons all-purpose flour**

In a large saucepan or Dutch oven brown meat, *half* at a time, in hot oil. Drain fat from pan. Stir in beef broth, wine, garlic, thyme, salt, pepper, and bay leaf. Bring to boiling. Reduce heat and simmer, covered, for 20 minutes.

Stir in squash, parsnips, sweet potatoes, celery, and onion. Return to boiling. Reduce heat and simmer, covered, about 30 minutes more or till vegetables are tender. Discard bay leaf.

In a small mixing bowl combine sour cream and flour. Stir *½ cup* of the hot liquid into the sour cream mixture. Return to saucepan. Cook and stir till thickened and bubbly. Cook and stir for 1 minute more. Makes 4 servings.

Nutrition information per serving: *368 calories, 23 g protein, 31 g carbohydrate, 13 g fat (6 g saturated), 70 mg cholesterol, 623 mg sodium, 945 mg potassium.*

SPICY SEAFOOD STEW

Orange roughy, cod, or haddock would be good choices for the fish in this full-bodied stew.

1 pound fresh *or* frozen fish fillets
   and/or fresh *or* frozen peeled and
   deveined shrimp
2 cups chicken broth *or* vegetable broth
1 cup sliced fresh mushrooms
1 cup sliced zucchini *or* yellow summer
   squash
½ cup chopped onion
1 clove garlic, minced
⅛ teaspoon salt
⅛ teaspoon crushed red pepper
1 bay leaf
2 14½-ounce cans Cajun-style stewed
   tomatoes
2 tablespoons snipped fresh parsley
½ teaspoon finely shredded lemon peel

Thaw fish and/or shrimp, if frozen. Cut fish into 1-inch pieces. In a large saucepan or Dutch oven combine chicken broth or vegetable broth, mushrooms, zucchini or yellow summer squash, onion, garlic, salt, crushed red pepper, and bay leaf. Bring to boiling. Reduce heat and simmer, covered, for 5 to 8 minutes or till vegetables are tender.

Stir in *undrained* tomatoes, fish, and shrimp. Bring just to boiling. Reduce heat and simmer, covered, for 2 to 3 minutes or till fish flakes easily with a fork and shrimp turn pink. Discard bay leaf.

In a small mixing bowl combine parsley and lemon peel; sprinkle atop each serving. Makes 4 servings.

Nutrition information per serving: 160 calories, 21 g protein, 19 g carbohydrate, 2 g fat (0 g saturated), 110 mg cholesterol, 1,318 mg sodium, 910 mg potassium.

NACHO CHEESE CHOWDER

Serve Nacho Cheese Chowder with tortilla chips for crunchy contrast.

½   pound ground beef
¾   cup chopped green pepper
¼   cup chopped onion
2   cups milk
1   11-ounce can condensed nacho cheese
      soup/dip
1   cup frozen whole kernel corn
1   medium tomato, chopped (¾ cup)
½   of an 8-ounce jar Mexican-style cheese
      spread (scant ½ cup)

In a large saucepan cook ground beef, green pepper, and onion till beef is brown and onion is tender. Drain fat from pan.

Stir in milk, soup/dip, corn, tomato, and cheese spread. Cook and stir over medium heat about 5 minutes or till heated through. Makes 4 servings.

Nutrition information per serving: 391 calories, 24 g protein, 28 g carbohydrate, 21 g fat (12 g saturated), 81 mg cholesterol, 1,178 mg sodium, 643 mg potassium.

CREAMY CLAM-SCALLOP CHOWDER

This luscious soup is bound to get your vote for one of the best-tasting seafood soups you've ever sipped.

6 ounces fresh *or* frozen bay scallops
1 pint shucked clams *or* two 6½-ounce
    cans minced clams
3 slices bacon, halved crosswise
2½ cups chopped, peeled potatoes
1 cup chopped shallots *or* finely
    chopped onion
1 tablespoon snipped fresh dill *or*
    1 teaspoon dried dillweed
1 teaspoon instant chicken bouillon
    granules
⅛ teaspoon pepper
2 cups milk
1 cup half-and-half *or* light cream
2 tablespoons all-purpose flour
¼ cup shredded carrot
2 tablespoons dry sherry
    Fresh dill (optional)

Thaw scallops, if frozen. Chop shucked clams, reserving juice; set clams aside. Strain clam juice to remove bits of shell. (*Or*, drain canned clams, reserving juice.) If necessary, add *water* to clam juice to equal 1 cup. Set clam juice mixture aside.

In a large saucepan or Dutch oven cook bacon till crisp. Remove bacon, reserving 1 tablespoon drippings, if desired. Drain bacon on paper towels; crumble. Set bacon aside.

In the same saucepan combine reserved bacon drippings (if desired), reserved clam juice mixture, potatoes, shallots or onion, dill, bouillon granules, and pepper. Bring to boiling. Reduce heat and simmer, covered, about 10 minutes or till potatoes are tender. With the back of a fork, mash potatoes slightly against the side of the pan.

Combine milk, half-and-half or light cream, and flour till smooth. Add to potato mixture along with shredded carrot. Cook and stir till slightly thickened and bubbly. Stir in clams and scallops. Return to boiling. Reduce heat; cook, uncovered, for 1 to 2 minutes more or till clams curl around the edges and scallops are opaque. Stir in sherry.

Sprinkle each serving with crumbled bacon and, if desired, garnish with additional dill. Makes 4 servings.

Nutrition information per serving: 420 calories, 31 g protein, 43 g carbohydrate, 13 g fat (7 g saturated), 86 mg cholesterol, 518 mg sodium, 1,273 mg potassium.

CRAB AND CAULIFLOWER CHOWDER

This richly flavored chowder would make an elegant first-course soup for 6 people. And, if you like, use broccoli flowerets instead of the cauliflower.

6   ounces fresh or frozen crabmeat *or* one 6-ounce can crabmeat, drained, flaked, and cartilage removed
2½ cups small cauliflower flowerets
¼   cup margarine *or* butter
¼   cup all-purpose flour
¼   teaspoon white pepper
2   cups chicken broth *or* vegetable broth
2   cups milk
1   3-ounce package cream cheese with chives, softened and cut up
¼   cup dry white wine
2   tablespoons snipped fresh parsley

Thaw crabmeat, if frozen. In a large saucepan cook cauliflower flowerets in margarine or butter for 5 to 6 minutes or just till crisp-tender.

Stir in flour and pepper. Add chicken broth or vegetable broth and milk all at once. Cook and stir till thickened and bubbly. Cook and stir for 1 minute more.

Gradually stir about *1 cup* of the hot milk mixture into the softened cream cheese; return to saucepan. Cook and stir over low heat till cream cheese melts. Stir in crabmeat and wine; heat through. Sprinkle each serving with parsley. Makes 4 servings.

Nutrition information per serving: 350 calories, 18 g protein, 16 g carbohydrate, 23 g fat (9 g saturated), 55 mg cholesterol, 1,108 mg sodium, 668 mg potassium.

CREAM OF SHRIMP SOUP

Dijon-style mustard seasons this fancy seafood soup.

3	cups vegetable broth *or* chicken broth
1½	cups loose-pack frozen peas and carrots
3	tablespoons thinly sliced green onion
⅛	teaspoon pepper
	Dash ground nutmeg
1	cup half-and-half *or* light cream
3	tablespoons all-purpose flour
8	ounces cooked, peeled and deveined shrimp, coarsely chopped
1	teaspoon Dijon-style mustard
	Snipped fresh parsley (optional)

In a large saucepan or Dutch oven combine vegetable broth or chicken broth, peas and carrots, green onion, pepper, and nutmeg. Bring to boiling. Reduce heat and simmer, covered, about 5 minutes or till vegetables are tender.

Meanwhile, gradually stir half-and-half or light cream into flour till smooth. Stir flour mixture into vegetable mixture. Cook and stir over medium heat till bubbly; cook and stir for 1 minute more. Stir in shrimp and mustard; heat through. If desired, garnish each serving with parsley. Makes 4 servings.

Nutrition information per serving: 186 calories, 16 g protein, 16 g carbohydrate, 9 g fat (5 g saturated), 133 mg cholesterol, 919 mg sodium, 290 mg potassium.

SHERRIED SALMON BISQUE

Salmon, shiitake mushrooms, leeks, and dry sherry come together to create a sophisticated soup.

12 ounces fresh *or* frozen salmon steaks,
      cut ¾ inch thick
 3 cups sliced fresh shiitake *or* other
      mushrooms
 ¾ cup thinly sliced leeks *or* ½ cup thinly
      sliced green onion
 2 tablespoons margarine *or* butter
 2 cups chicken broth *or* vegetable broth
1½ teaspoons snipped fresh dill *or*
      ½ teaspoon dried dillweed
      Dash pepper
 2 cups half-and-half *or* light cream
 2 tablespoons cornstarch
 2 tablespoons dry sherry
      Fresh dill (optional)

Thaw salmon, if frozen, and cut into ¾-inch pieces. Discard skin and bones. In a large saucepan cook mushrooms and leeks or green onion in margarine or butter till tender. Stir in chicken broth or vegetable broth, dill, and pepper. Bring to boiling.

Combine half-and-half or light cream and cornstarch; stir into mushroom mixture. Cook and stir over medium heat till thickened and bubbly. Add salmon; simmer, covered, about 4 minutes or till fish flakes easily. Gently stir in the dry sherry. If desired, garnish with additional dill. Makes 4 servings.

Nutrition information per serving: 358 calories, 20 g protein, 16 g carbohydrate, 23 g fat (11 g saturated), 60 mg cholesterol, 562 mg sodium, 622 mg potassium.

FISH-ASPARAGUS BISQUE

Serve this thick, velvety soup with a crisp vegetable salad and an assortment of crackers.

½ pound fresh *or* frozen cod *or* orange
     roughy fillets
1 cup sliced leeks *or* chopped onion
1 cup sliced fresh shiitake mushrooms
     or button mushrooms
½ pound asparagus spears, cut into
     1-inch pieces (1 cup) *or* ½ of a
     10-ounce package frozen cut
     asparagus, thawed
1 clove garlic, minced
¼ cup margarine *or* butter
¼ cup all-purpose flour
1 teaspoon snipped fresh thyme *or*
     ¼ teaspoon dried thyme, crushed
1 teaspoon snipped fresh savory *or*
     ¼ teaspoon dried savory, crushed
1 14½-ounce can chicken broth
1¾ cups milk
½ cup shredded Jarlsberg cheese *or* Swiss
     cheese (2 ounces)

Thaw fish, if frozen. Cut fish into ¾-inch pieces. In a large saucepan or Dutch oven cook leeks or onion, mushrooms, asparagus, and garlic in margarine or butter for 6 to 8 minutes or till vegetables are crisp-tender. Stir in flour, thyme, and savory. Add chicken broth and milk all at once. Cook and stir till thickened and bubbly. Cook and stir for 1 minute more.

Add the fish. Bring to boiling. Reduce heat and simmer, uncovered, for 3 to 5 minutes more or till fish flakes easily with a fork. Stir in cheese. Makes 4 servings.

Nutrition information per serving: 324 calories, 22 g protein, 17 g carbohydrate, 19 g fat (6 g saturated), 43 mg cholesterol, 614 mg sodium, 649 mg potassium.

HALIBUT CHOWDER WITH SPINACH

Cod, pike, or orange roughy fillets would all make good substitutes for the halibut in this flavor-packed chowder.

1   pound fresh *or* frozen halibut steaks,
       cut ¾-inch thick
4   slices bacon, halved crosswise
2½ cups chopped, peeled potatoes
1   cup sliced leeks *or* chopped onion
1   8-ounce bottle clam juice
½   cup chicken broth
1½ teaspoons snipped fresh dill *or*
       ½ teaspoon dried dillweed
¼   teaspoon salt
¼   teaspoon white pepper
1½ cups half-and-half *or* light cream
1   cup milk
2   tablespoons all-purpose flour
3   cups chopped spinach *or* ½ of a
       10-ounce package frozen chopped
       spinach, thawed and well drained

Thaw halibut steaks, if frozen, and cut into ¾-inch cubes. Discard skin and bones. In a large saucepan cook bacon till crisp. Remove bacon, reserving 1 tablespoon drippings, if desired. Drain bacon on paper towels; crumble bacon and set aside.

In the same saucepan combine reserved bacon drippings (if desired), potatoes, leeks or onion, clam juice, chicken broth, dill, salt, and pepper. Bring to boiling. Reduce heat and simmer, covered, about 15 minutes or till potatoes are tender. With the back of a fork, mash potatoes slightly against the side of the pan.

Combine half-and-half, milk, and flour till smooth; add to potato mixture. Cook and stir just till mixture comes to boiling; add halibut. Reduce heat and simmer, uncovered, for 3 to 4 minutes or till fish flakes easily with a fork.

Stir in spinach. Cook 1 to 2 minutes more or just till spinach is wilted. Sprinkle each serving with crumbled bacon. Makes 4 servings.

Nutrition information per serving: 431 calories, 35 g protein, 33 g carbohydrate, 18 g fat (9 g saturated), 80 mg cholesterol, 630 mg sodium, 1,366 mg potassium.

MANHATTAN FISH CHOWDER

Manhattan-style chowders are tomato-based and may contain other vegetables in place of the potatoes found in milk-based New England-style chowders.

¾ pound fresh *or* frozen fish fillets
1 24-ounce can vegetable juice cocktail
1 11-ounce can whole kernel corn with
    sweet peppers
½ cup sliced green onion
¼ cup chicken broth
1½ teaspoons snipped fresh thyme *or*
    ½ teaspoon dried thyme, crushed
1 teaspoon Worcestershire sauce
    Several dashes bottled hot pepper
    sauce

Thaw fish, if frozen. Cut fish into ¾-inch pieces. In a large saucepan combine vegetable juice cocktail, corn, green onion, chicken broth, thyme, Worcestershire sauce, and hot pepper sauce. Bring to boiling. Reduce heat and simmer, covered, for 8 minutes.

Add fish to saucepan. Return to boiling. Reduce heat and simmer, covered, for 3 to 5 minutes more or till fish flakes easily with a fork, stirring once. Makes 4 servings.

Nutrition information per serving: 164 calories, 16 g protein, 22 g carbohydrate, 1 g fat (0 g saturated), 34 mg cholesterol, 995 mg sodium, 690 mg potassium.

TURKEY-BARLEY CHOWDER

This chill-chasing chowder is guaranteed to keep winter at bay.

3   cups chicken broth
3   carrots, cut into julienne strips
      (2 cups)
1   cup sliced leeks *or* chopped onion
¾   cup quick-cooking barley
1½ teaspoons snipped fresh savory *or*
      ½ teaspoon dried savory, crushed
¼   teaspoon pepper
⅛   teaspoon salt
2   cups half-and-half *or* light cream
1½ cups chopped cooked turkey *or*
      chicken
1   4-ounce jar strained carrot baby food
      Snipped fresh savory (optional)

In a large saucepan or Dutch oven combine chicken broth, carrot strips, leeks or onion, barley, savory, pepper, and salt. Bring to boiling. Reduce heat and simmer, covered, about 15 minutes or till vegetables are tender.

Stir in half-and-half or light cream, turkey or chicken, and strained carrots. Heat through. If desired, garnish each serving with additional savory. Makes 4 servings.

Nutrition information per serving: 445 calories, 27 g protein, 43 g carbohydrate, 18 g fat (10 g saturated), 85 mg cholesterol, 787 mg sodium, 758 mg potassium.

TEX-MEX CREAM OF CHICKEN SOUP

Ground red pepper and green chili peppers add a spiciness to this creamy soup. For an accompaniment, serve some cornbread or cornsticks with it.

½   **pound ground raw chicken** *or* **turkey**
¼   **cup chopped onion**
2   **cloves garlic, minced**
2   **cups milk**
1   **10¾-ounce can condensed cream of chicken soup**
1   **7-ounce can whole kernel corn with sweet peppers, drained**
1   **medium tomato, chopped (¾ cup)**
1   **4-ounce can diced green chili peppers, drained**
2   **tablespoons snipped fresh cilantro** *or* **parsley**
¼   **teaspoon ground red pepper**
1   **cup shredded Monterey Jack cheese (4 ounces)**
    Fresh cilantro *or* **parsley (optional)**

In a large saucepan or Dutch oven cook ground chicken or turkey, onion, and garlic till chicken or turkey is no longer pink and onion is tender but not brown. Drain fat from pan.

Stir in milk, cream of chicken soup, corn, chopped tomato, chili peppers, cilantro or parsley, and ground red pepper. Bring to boiling. Reduce heat and simmer, uncovered, for 5 minutes, stirring occasionally. Add cheese; cook and stir till cheese melts. Garnish each serving with additional cilantro or parsley, if desired. Makes 4 servings.

Nutrition information per serving: 375 calories, 24 g protein, 29 g carbohydrate, 19 g fat (9 g saturated), 68 mg cholesterol, 1,481 mg sodium, 681 mg .potassium.

EASY CHEESY VEGETABLE-CHICKEN CHOWDER

This hearty chowder lives up to its name. It's easy—only takes about 20 minutes to cook—and with a cup of cheddar cheese, it's definately cheesy!

1   cup small broccoli flowerets
1   cup frozen loose-pack whole kernel
      corn
½   cup water
¼   cup chopped onion
1½ teaspoons snipped fresh thyme *or*
      ½ teaspoon dried thyme, crushed
2   cups milk
1½ cups chopped cooked chicken *or*
      turkey
1   10¾-ounce can condensed cream of
      potato soup
¾   cup shredded cheddar cheese
      (3 ounces)
    Dash pepper
¼   cup shredded cheddar cheese
      (1 ounce)

In a large saucepan combine broccoli, corn, water, onion, and thyme. Bring to boiling. Reduce heat and simmer, covered, for 8 to 10 minutes or till vegetables are tender. Do not drain.

Stir milk, chicken or turkey, potato soup, the ¾ cup cheddar cheese, and pepper into vegetable mixture. Cook and stir over medium heat till cheese melts and mixture is heated through. Sprinkle each serving with the remaining cheddar cheese. Makes 4 servings.

Nutrition information per serving: 380 calories, 31 g protein, 25 g carbohydrate, 18 g fat (9 g saturated), 94 mg cholesterol, 970 mg sodium, 630 mg potassium.

CREAMY BROCCOLI-CHICKEN SOUP

This incredibly creamy soup is packed with vegetables, poultry, and just the right amount of seasoning.

1½ cups small broccoli flowerets
1 cup sliced fresh mushrooms
½ cup shredded carrot
¼ cup chopped onion
¼ cup margarine *or* butter
¼ cup all-purpose flour
1½ teaspoons snipped fresh basil *or*
     ½ teaspoon dried basil, crushed
¼ teaspoon pepper
3 cups milk
1 cup half-and-half *or* light cream
1 tablespoon white wine Worcestershire
     sauce
1½ teaspoons instant chicken bouillon
     granules
1½ cups chopped cooked chicken *or*
     turkey

In a medium saucepan cook and stir broccoli, mushrooms, carrot, and onion in margarine or butter for 6 to 8 minutes or till vegetables are tender but not brown.

Stir in flour, basil, and pepper. Add milk and half-and-half or light cream all at once; add Worcestershire sauce and bouillon granules. Cook and stir till thickened and bubbly. Stir in chicken or turkey; heat through. Makes 4 servings.

Nutrition information per serving: 441 calories, 28 g protein, 24 g carbohydrate, 27 g fat (10 g saturated), 86 mg cholesterol, 675 mg sodium, 822 mg potassium.

WINTER SQUASH BISQUE

Butternut or buttercup squash works equally as well in this surprisingly sweet, autumn soup. Use 1½ pounds and save any remaining squash for another use.

1   **medium acorn squash (about 1½ pounds)**
2   **cups chicken broth**
¼   **teaspoon ground ginger**
⅛   **teaspoon salt**
⅛   **teaspoon pepper**
    Dash ground cinnamon
1   **cup half-and-half *or* light cream**
¼   **cup dairy sour cream (optional)**
    Fresh chives (optional)

Halve squash; remove seeds. Cut each piece in half. Place a steamer basket in a large saucepan or Dutch oven; add broth to saucepan. Bring to boiling; place squash in steamer basket.

Cover and steam for 25 to 30 minutes or till squash can be pierced easily with a fork. Carefully remove steamer basket from saucepan. Reserve steaming liquid in saucepan.

Using a spoon, scoop squash pulp out of the peel; discard peel. Place squash pulp in a blender container or food processor bowl. Cover and blend or process till mixture is smooth, adding as much of the reserved liquid as necessary.

Stir pureed squash into remaining reserved liquid in the saucepan; stir in ginger, salt, pepper, and cinnamon. Bring mixture to boiling. Reduce heat and stir in half-and-half or cream. Heat through. If desired, garnish each serving with a dollop of sour cream and chives. Makes 4 servings.

Nutrition information per serving: *156 calories, 6 g protein, 18 g carbohydrate, 8 g fat (5 g saturated), 22 mg cholesterol, 485 mg sodium, 591 mg potassium.*

MEXICAN CORN CHOWDER

This simple chowder, along with a sandwich or salad, makes a great supper on a chilly winter night.

2   cups cut fresh corn *or* one 10-ounce
        package frozen whole kernel corn
½   cup cubed, peeled potato
½   cup chopped green pepper
½   cup water
¼   cup chopped onion
2   teaspoons instant chicken bouillon
        granules
½   teaspoon ground cumin
2½ cups milk
3   tablespoons all-purpose flour
1   4-ounce can diced green chili peppers
    Fresh cilantro *or* parsley sprigs
        (optional)
    Chopped tomato (optional)

In a large saucepan combine corn, potato, green pepper, water, onion, bouillon granules, and cumin. Bring to boiling. Reduce heat and simmer, covered, about 8 minutes or till corn and potatoes are tender. Do not drain.

Stir together milk and flour; stir into corn mixture. Add green chili peppers. Cook and stir till thickened and bubbly. Cook and stir for 1 minute more. If desired, garnish with cilantro or parsley and chopped tomato. Makes 4 to 6 servings.

Nutrition information per serving: 168 calories, 8 g protein, 28 g carbohydrate, 4 g fat (2 g saturated), 11 mg cholesterol, 518 mg sodium, 485 mg potassium.

BAKED POTATO SOUP

Speed up the preparation time by cooking the potatoes in your microwave oven.

2 large baking potatoes (8 ounces each)
3 tablespoons thinly sliced green onion
⅓ cup margarine *or* butter
⅓ cup all-purpose flour
2 teaspoons snipped fresh dill *or*
    ¼ teaspoon dried dillweed
¼ teaspoon salt
¼ teaspoon pepper
4 cups milk
¾ cup shredded American cheese
    (3 ounces)
3 tablespoons thinly sliced green onion
4 slices bacon, crisp-cooked, drained,
    and crumbled

Scrub potatoes thoroughly with a brush; pat dry. Prick potatoes with a fork. Bake in a 425° oven for 40 to 60 minutes or till tender. Let cool. Cut potatoes in half lengthwise; gently scoop out each potato. Discard potato skins.

In a large saucepan cook 3 tablespoons green onion in margarine or butter till tender; stir in flour, dill, salt, and pepper. Add milk all at once. Cook and stir till thickened and bubbly. Cook and stir for 1 minute more. Add the potato pulp and *½ cup* of the shredded cheese; stir till cheese melts.

Garnish each serving with the remaining shredded cheese, 3 tablespoons green onion, and bacon. Makes 6 servings.

Nutrition information per serving: 324 calories, 12 g protein, 25 g carbohydrate, 20 g fat (7 g saturated), 29 mg cholesterol, 561 mg sodium, 514 mg potassium.

BUTTERMILK-PEA POTAGE

To make the bleeding heart garnish, dollop a small amount of yogurt or sour cream at regular intervals on the soup. Run the tip of a knife or a skewer through each drop, creating the heart shapes.

1   14½-ounce can chicken broth
2   cups shelled peas *or* one 10-ounce
      package frozen peas
1   cup torn spinach
¼   cup chopped onion
2   teaspoons snipped fresh savory *or* dill
      or ¼ teaspoon dried savory, crushed,
      or dillweed
2   teaspoons cornstarch
1   cup buttermilk
    Fresh savory *or* dill (optional)

In a medium saucepan combine chicken broth, peas, spinach, onion, and savory or dill. Bring to boiling. Reduce heat and simmer, covered, for 10 to 15 minutes (5 to 6 minutes for frozen peas) or till peas are very tender. Cool mixture slightly.

Place *half* of the pea mixture and the cornstarch in a blender container or food processor bowl. Cover and blend or process till smooth. Repeat with remaining pea mixture. Return all the pea mixture to saucepan. Cook and stir till thickened and bubbly. Cook and stir for 1 minute more. Stir in buttermilk; heat through.

Ladle soup into bowls. If desired, garnish with additional savory or dill. Makes 4 servings.

Nutrition information per serving: 118 calories, 9 g protein, 18 g carbohydrate, 1 g fat (1 g saturated), 2 mg cholesterol, 497 mg sodium, 419 mg potassium.

AUTUMN PEAR AND PUMPKIN SOUP

First there was pumpkin pie, then pumpkin cookies, and now pumpkin soup! The uses for this hard-shelled squash seem never ending.

½   cup chopped onion
½   cup water
2   teaspoons instant chicken bouillon
      granules
1   16-ounce can pumpkin
2½   cups half-and-half *or* light cream
1¾   cups pear nectar
¼   teaspoon ground ginger
¼   teaspoon white pepper
      Pear slices (optional)

In a large saucepan combine onion, water, and bouillon granules. Bring to boiling. Reduce heat and simmer, covered, about 10 minutes or till onion is very tender; cool slightly.

Transfer mixture to a blender container or food processor bowl. Add pumpkin. Cover and blend or process till smooth. Return pumpkin mixture to saucepan. Stir in half-and-half or light cream, pear nectar, ginger, and white pepper. Cook and stir till heated through.

Ladle into soup bowls. If desired, garnish each serving with pear slices. Makes 6 servings.

Nutrition information per serving: 210 calories, 4 g protein, 24 g carbohydrate, 12 g fat (7 g saturated), 37 mg cholesterol, 337 mg sodium, 334 mg potassium.

SHIITAKE MUSHROOM-TOMATO BISQUE

If fresh shiitake mushrooms aren't available, soak dried ones in hot water. Two ounces of the dried mushrooms equal 1 cup of the fresh.

½ cup sliced leeks *or* chopped onion
½ cup sliced celery
2 cloves garlic, minced
2 tablespoons margarine *or* butter
1½ cups sliced fresh shiitake *or* other mushrooms
1 16-ounce can tomatoes, cut up
1½ cups chicken broth *or* vegetable broth
¼ cup whipping cream
1 tablespoon snipped fresh dill *or* 1 teaspoon dried dillweed
Dash pepper
½ cup sliced fresh shiitake *or* other mushrooms
1 tablespoon margarine *or* butter
Fresh dill (optional)

In a large saucepan or Dutch oven cook sliced leeks or chopped onion, celery, and garlic in the 2 tablespoons margarine or butter till tender. Add the 1½ cups mushrooms and cook about 5 minutes more or till mushrooms are tender. Stir in *undrained* canned tomatoes, chicken or vegetable broth, whipping cream, dill, and pepper. Bring to boiling. Reduce heat and simmer, covered, for 30 minutes. Cool mixture slightly.

Place *half* of the tomato mixture in a blender container or food processor bowl. Cover and blend or process till smooth. Repeat with remaining tomato mixture. Return all the tomato mixture to saucepan and heat through.

Meanwhile, in a small skillet cook the ½ cup mushrooms in the 1 tablespoon margarine or butter about 5 minutes or till tender. To serve, ladle bisque into serving bowls. Garnish with cooked mushrooms and, if desired, additional dill. Makes 4 servings.

Nutrition information per serving: 184 calories, 4 g protein, 10 g carbohydrate, 15 g fat (5 g saturated), 20 mg cholesterol, 608 mg sodium, 551 mg potassium.

ORIENTAL HOT-AND-SOUR SOUP

This Chinese specialty is delightfully peppery and vinegary.

8 ounces fresh *or* frozen peeled and
    deveined shrimp
3½ cups chicken broth
1 7-ounce jar whole straw mushrooms,
    drained and halved lengthwise
    (optional)
¼ cup rice vinegar *or* white vinegar
2 tablespoons soy sauce
1 teaspoon sugar
1 teaspoon grated gingerroot
½ teaspoon pepper
4 ounces tofu (fresh bean curd), cut into
    bite-size pieces
1 tablespoon cornstarch
1 tablespoon cold water
1 cup fresh pea pods, halved crosswise,
    or ½ of a 6-ounce package frozen
    pea pods, thawed and halved
    crosswise
1 beaten egg
2 tablespoons thinly sliced green onion

Thaw shrimp, if frozen. In a large saucepan or Dutch oven combine chicken broth, mushrooms (if desired), rice vinegar or white vinegar, soy sauce, sugar, gingerroot, and pepper. Bring to boiling. Reduce heat and simmer, covered, for 2 minutes.

Add shrimp and tofu. Simmer, covered, for 1 minute more. Stir together cornstarch and cold water. Stir into chicken broth mixture along with pea pods. Cook and stir till slightly thickened and bubbly. Cook and stir for 2 minutes more. Pour the egg into the soup in a steady stream while stirring 2 or 3 times to create shreds. Remove from heat. Stir in green onion. Makes 6 servings.

Nutrition information per serving: 117 calories, 14 g protein, 7 g carbohydrate, 4 g fat (1 g saturated), 94 mg cholesterol, 877 mg sodium, 311 mg potassium.

WILD RICE-MUSHROOM SOUP

A great soup for entertaining—it's exceptionally easy, but very special because of the wild rice and sherry.

3   cups chicken broth
⅓   cup wild rice
½   cup sliced green onion
1   cup half-and-half *or* light cream
2   tablespoons all-purpose flour
1   teaspoon snipped fresh thyme *or*
     ¼ teaspoon dried thyme, crushed
⅛   teaspoon pepper
½   cup sliced fresh mushrooms
1   tablespoon dry sherry

In a medium saucepan combine chicken broth and uncooked wild rice. Bring to boiling. Reduce heat and simmer, covered, for 40 minutes. Stir in green onion and cook for 5 to 10 minutes more or till the rice is tender.

Combine half-and-half or light cream, flour, thyme, and pepper. Stir into rice mixture along with mushrooms. Cook and stir till thickened and bubbly. Cook and stir for 1 minute more. Stir in sherry and heat through. Makes 4 servings.

Nutrition information per serving: 177 calories, 8 g protein, 17 g carbohydrate, 8 g fat (5 g saturated), 22 mg cholesterol, 608 mg sodium, 346 mg potassium.

LEEK-GRUYÈRE CREAM SOUP

Leeks are a member of the onion family that resemble an overgrown green onion with overlapping, wide, green leaves; a fat, white stalk; and shaggy roots at the bulb end. Leeks have a subtle onion flavor.

6   cups chicken broth
4   cups sliced leeks
1   cup sliced fresh mushrooms
1   teaspoon fines herbes, crushed
½   teaspoon white pepper
⅓   cup all-purpose flour
1½ cups shredded process Gruyère cheese
       (6 ounces)
2   tablespoons snipped fresh parsley
1   cup whipping cream
       Thinly sliced leeks (optional)

In a large kettle or Dutch oven combine *4 cups* of the chicken broth, leeks, mushrooms, fines herbes, and pepper. Bring to boiling. Reduce heat and simmer, covered, for 10 to 15 minutes or till leeks are tender. Cool slightly.

Place *one-third* of the leek mixture in a blender container or food processor bowl. Cover and blend or process till smooth. Repeat with remaining leek mixture. Return all of the smooth leek mixture to the kettle or Dutch oven; stir in *1 cup* of the remaining chicken broth.

Combine the remaining *1 cup* of the chicken broth and the flour till smooth. Stir into hot broth mixture along with shredded cheese and parsley. Cook and stir till slightly thickened and bubbly and cheese melts. Stir in whipping cream; heat through.

If desired, garnish with additional sliced leeks. Makes 8 servings.

Nutrition information per serving: 193 calories, 7 g protein, 11 g carbohydrate, 14 g fat (8 g saturated), 47 mg cholesterol, 618 mg sodium, 282 mg potassium.

SHIITAKE MUSHROOM AND SPINACH BROTH

Look for shiitake mushrooms, a Japanese variety, in gourmet markets or near other oriental products in your grocery store.

7   to 8 dried shiitake mushrooms *or* other dried mushrooms
4   14½-ounce cans chicken broth
1   large carrot, sliced
2   tablespoons minced dried onion
1   tablespoon lemon juice
1½ teaspoons snipped fresh basil *or* ½ teaspoon dried basil, crushed
⅛   teaspoon garlic powder
1½ cups torn spinach *or* watercress

In a small bowl soak mushrooms in enough hot *water* to cover for 30 minutes. Rinse well and squeeze to drain thoroughly. Thinly slice mushrooms, discarding stems.

In a large saucepan or kettle combine mushrooms, broth, sliced carrot, dried onion, lemon juice, basil, and garlic powder. Bring to boiling. Reduce heat and simmer, covered, for 8 to 10 minutes or till carrot is almost tender, stirring occasionally.

Stir in spinach or watercress. Simmer, covered, about 2 minutes more or till spinach wilts. Makes 8 servings.

Nutrition information per serving: 61 calories, 5 g protein, 7 g carbohydrate, 1 g fat (0 g saturated), 0 mg cholesterol, 725 mg sodium, 365 mg potassium.

FRESH TOMATO SOUP

A touch of lime juice adds a refreshing twist to this favorite soup.

3 medium tomatoes, peeled and
    quartered *or* one 16-ounce can
    tomatoes, cut up
1½ cups water
½ cup chopped onion
½ cup chopped celery
½ of a 6-ounce can (⅓ cup) tomato paste
1 tablespoon snipped fresh parsley
2 teaspoons instant chicken bouillon
    granules
2 teaspoons lime juice *or* lemon juice
1 teaspoon sugar
    Few dashes bottled hot pepper sauce
    Snipped fresh parsley (optional)

If desired, seed the fresh tomatoes. In a large saucepan combine fresh tomatoes or *undrained* canned tomatoes, water, onion, celery, tomato paste, parsley, chicken bouillon granules, lime juice or lemon juice, sugar, and hot pepper sauce. Bring to boiling. Reduce heat and simmer, covered, about 20 minutes or till celery and onion are very tender. Cool the mixture slightly.

Place *one-third* of the mixture in a blender container. Cover and blend till smooth. (Or, place *half* of the mixture in a food processor bowl. Cover and process till smooth.) Repeat with the remaining mixture. Return all of the mixture to the saucepan; heat through.

If desired, garnish with additional parsley. Makes 4 servings.

Nutrition information per serving: 61 calories, 3 g protein, 13 g carbohydrate, 1 g fat, (0 g saturated), 0 mg cholesterol, 474 mg sodium, 542 mg potassium.

GUACAMOLE SOUP

Each chilly sip of this no-cook, avocado soup will refresh your taste buds.

1½ cups chicken broth
1 cup half-and-half *or* light cream
1 large avocado, seeded, peeled, and
      sliced
2 tablespoons salsa
1 tablespoon snipped fresh cilantro *or*
      parsley
1 tablespoon lemon juice
¼ cup thinly sliced green onion
⅛ teaspoon salt
⅛ teaspoon pepper
   Several dashes bottled hot pepper
      sauce
   Lime wedges
¼ cup dairy sour cream
¼ cup finely chopped tomato

In a medium mixing bowl combine broth, half-and-half or light cream, avocado, salsa, cilantro or parsley, lemon juice, *half* of the green onion, salt, pepper, and bottled hot pepper sauce. Place *half* of the mixture into a blender container or food processor bowl. Cover and blend or process till smooth. Repeat with remaining mixture.

Cover and chill for up to 6 hours. Garnish each serving with lime wedges, sour cream, chopped tomato, and remaining sliced green onion. Makes 4 servings.

Nutrition information per serving: 225 calories, 6 g protein, 10 g carbohydrate, 20 g fat (8 g saturated), 29 mg cholesterol, 426 mg sodium, 596 mg potassium.

CHILLED CARROT SOUP

Cold soups like this one are a real advantage when you're entertaining. They can be made the night before and chilled till serving time.

1   pound carrots, chopped
½   cup water
1   14½-ounce can chicken broth
¼   teaspoon white pepper
     Dash ground ginger
½   of an 8-ounce carton dairy sour cream
     Celery leaves (optional)

In a medium saucepan cook carrots in water for 15 to 20 minutes or till very tender. Drain in a colander. Transfer carrots to a blender container or food processor bowl. Cover and blend or process till carrots are smooth.

Transfer carrots to a large mixing bowl. Stir in chicken broth, white pepper, and ground ginger. Cover and chill for 2 to 24 hours.

Before serving, stir in sour cream. Top each serving with celery leaves, if desired. Makes 4 to 6 servings.

Nutrition information per serving: 127 calories, 4 g protein, 13 g carbohydrate, 7 g fat (4 g saturated), 13 mg cholesterol, 440 mg sodium, 384 mg potassium.

GAZPACHO

With only 1 gram of fat and no cholesterol, this chilled soup is a great, heart-healthy way to enjoy an abundant summer crop of tomatoes, cucumbers, and green peppers.

1 cup chicken broth
2 medium oranges, peeled
2 medium tomatoes, peeled and chopped
1 6-ounce can tomato juice
⅓ cup chopped, seeded cucumber
2 tablespoons finely chopped green pepper
1 shallot, finely chopped
1 tablespoon snipped fresh basil *or* 1 teaspoon dried basil, crushed
1 tablespoon red wine vinegar
1 clove garlic, minced
⅛ teaspoon ground red pepper
Dash ground black pepper
Fresh basil (optional)

Chill chicken broth; skim off any fat. Section oranges, working over a bowl to catch juices. Cut sections into bite-size pieces.

In a large mixing bowl combine orange pieces and reserved orange juice, tomatoes, tomato juice, cucumber, green pepper, shallot, basil, wine vinegar, garlic, ground red pepper, and black pepper. Add broth; stir till thoroughly combined. Cover and chill for 2 to 24 hours.

To serve, ladle into chilled soup bowls or mugs. If desired, garnish with additional basil. Makes 4 to 6 servings.

Nutrition information per serving: 50 calories, 3 g protein, 10 g carbohydrate, 1 g fat (0 g saturated), 0 mg cholesterol, 366 mg sodium, 379 mg potassium.

CHILLED POTATO SOUP

Another elegant garnish for this sophisticated soup is some fresh dill and a chilled, cooked asparagus spear.

2   cups water
2   cups cubed, peeled potatoes
½   cup sliced green onion
1   tablespoon instant chicken bouillon
      granules
1½   teaspoons snipped fresh tarragon *or*
      ½ teaspoon dried tarragon, crushed
1   clove garlic, minced
⅛   teaspoon pepper
1   cup buttermilk
      Fresh tarragon *or* fresh savory
      (optional)

In a large saucepan combine water, potatoes, green onion, chicken bouillon granules, tarragon, garlic, and pepper. Bring to boiling. Reduce heat and simmer, covered, for 20 to 25 minutes or till potatoes are very tender. Cool.

Drain the potatoes, reserving the liquid. Mash potatoes. Gradually stir in the reserved liquid. Stir in the buttermilk. Transfer mixture to a bowl; cover and chill for 4 to 24 hours.

To serve, ladle chilled soup into bowls. If desired, garnish each serving with additional tarragon or savory. Makes 6 to 8 servings.

Nutrition information per serving: 69 calories, 3 g protein, 14 g carbohydrate, 1 g fat (0 g saturated), 2 mg cholesterol, 481 mg sodium, 279 mg potassium.

MIXED FRUIT SOUP

If you like, serve this Swedish dessert soup with a dollop of vanilla yogurt.

½   of an 8-ounce package (about ¾ cup)
       mixed dried fruit
1½ cups water
¼   cup dried cherries *or* dried cranberries
¼   cup light raisins
2   inches stick cinnamon
⅔   cup unsweetened white grape juice
2   teaspoons quick-cooking tapioca
⅛   teaspoon ground nutmeg
3   tablespoons currant jelly

Pit prunes, if necessary, and cut up any large pieces of fruit. In a medium saucepan combine mixed dried fruit, water, dried cherries or dried cranberries, raisins, and cinnamon. Bring to boiling. Reduce heat and simmer, covered, for 10 minutes.

Meanwhile, stir together white grape juice, tapioca, and nutmeg; let stand for 5 minutes. Stir tapioca mixture into cooked fruit mixture along with jelly. Bring to boiling. Reduce heat and simmer, covered, for 5 minutes, stirring occasionally. Remove stick cinnamon.

Serve warm or chilled. Makes 4 or 5 servings.

Nutrition information per serving: 196 calories, 2 g protein, 50 g carbohydrate, 0 g fat (0 g saturated), 0 mg cholesterol, 12 mg sodium, 372 mg potassium.

CHILLED PEACH-YOGURT SOUP

This refreshing, cool soup works as an appetizer or dessert.

2   cups sliced, peeled peaches *or* frozen
    unsweetened peach slices
¾   cup peach *or* apricot nectar
1½ teaspoons lemon juice
¼   teaspoon ground cinnamon
1   8-ounce carton vanilla yogurt
    Fresh mint sprigs (optional)
    Raspberries (optional)

Thaw peaches, if frozen. *Do not* drain. Place peach slices, peach or apricot nectar, lemon juice, and cinnamon in a blender container or food processor bowl. Cover and blend or process till smooth.

If desired, reserve 2 tablespoons of the yogurt for garnish. In a large mixing bowl stir a little of the peach mixture into the remaining yogurt, stirring till smooth. Stir in the remaining peach mixture.

Cover and chill for 2 to 24 hours. If desired, garnish with the reserved yogurt, mint sprigs, and raspberries. Makes 4 servings.

Nutrition information per serving: 123 calories, 4 g protein, 26 g carbohydrate, 1 g fat (0 g saturated), 3 mg cholesterol, 43 mg sodium, 319 mg potassium.

STRAWBERRY-MELON SOUP WITH GINGER MELON BALLS

This tangy, chilled soup is the perfect way to start a springtime brunch.

1   small cantaloupe
½   of a small honeydew melon
½   cup unsweetened pineapple juice
⅓   cup sugar
1   tablespoon grated gingerroot
4   cups fresh *or* frozen unsweetened
     strawberries
1   8-ounce carton vanilla yogurt
1   8-ounce carton dairy sour cream
2   cups milk
     Carnation petals (optional)

Using a small melon baller, scoop the cantaloupe and the honeydew into balls or use a knife to cut melons into cubes. (You should have about 4 cups cantaloupe and 2 cups honeydew.) Set melon aside.

In a small saucepan combine pineapple juice, sugar, and gingerroot. Bring to boiling, stirring till sugar dissolves. Reduce heat and simmer, uncovered, over medium heat for 5 to 7 minutes or till the mixture is the consistency of a thin syrup. Remove from heat; cool. Transfer syrup to a storage container. Add *2 cups* of the cantaloupe pieces and all of the honeydew pieces. Cover and chill overnight.

Meanwhile, in a blender container or food processor bowl cover and blend or process strawberries till smooth; remove and set aside. Cover and blend or process remaining *2 cups* cantaloupe pieces till smooth. In a large mixing bowl stir together yogurt and sour cream. Add pureed strawberries, pureed melon, and milk; stir till combined. Cover and chill overnight.

To serve, drain melon balls, reserving syrup; stir reserved syrup into chilled soup. Ladle soup into bowls; top with melon balls. If desired, garnish each serving with carnation petals. Makes 8 to 10 servings.

Nutrition information per serving: 211 calories, 5 g protein, 34 g carbohydrate, 8 g fat (4 g saturated), 17 mg cholesterol, 63 mg sodium, 663 mg potassium.

Keep track of your daily nutrition needs by using the information we provide at the end of each recipe. We've analyzed the nutritional content of each recipe serving for you. When a recipe gives an ingredient substitution, we used the first choice in the analysis. If it makes a range of servings (such as 4 to 6), we used the smallest number. Ingredients listed as optional weren't included in the calculations.

METRIC COOKING HINTS

By making a few conversions, cooks in Australia, Canada, and the United Kingdom can use the recipes in Better Homes and Gardens® *Soups and Stews* with confidence. The charts on this page provide a guide for converting measurements from the U.S. customary system, which is used throughout this book, to the imperial and metric systems. There also is a conversion table for oven temperatures to accommodate the differences in oven calibrations.

Volume and Weight: Americans traditionally use cup measures for liquid and solid ingredients. The chart (top right) shows the approximate imperial and metric equivalents. If you are accustomed to weighing solid ingredients, here are some helpful approximate equivalents.

■ 1 cup butter, caster sugar, or rice = 8 ounces = about 250 grams
■ 1 cup flour = 4 ounces = about 125 grams
■ 1 cup icing sugar = 5 ounces = about 150 grams

Spoon measures are used for smaller amounts of ingredients. Although the size of the tablespoon varies slightly among countries, for practical purposes and for recipes in this book, a straight substitution is all that's necessary.

Measurements made using cups or spoons should always be level, unless stated otherwise.

Product Differences: Most of the ingredients called for in the recipes in this book are available in English-speaking countries. However, some are known by different names. Here are some common American ingredients and their possible counterparts:

■ Sugar is granulated or caster sugar.
■ Powdered sugar is icing sugar.
■ All-purpose flour is plain household flour or white flour. When self-rising flour is used in place of all-purpose flour in a recipe that calls for leavening, omit the leavening agent (baking soda or baking powder) and salt.
■ Light corn syrup is golden syrup.
■ Cornstarch is cornflour.
■ Baking soda is bicarbonate of soda.
■ Vanilla is vanilla essence.

USEFUL EQUIVALENTS

⅛ teaspoon = 0.5ml
¼ teaspoon = 1ml
½ teaspoon = 2 ml
1 teaspoon = 5 ml
¼ cup = 2 fluid ounces = 50ml
⅓ cup = 3 fluid ounces = 75ml
½ cup = 4 fluid ounces = 125ml

⅔ cup = 5 fluid ounces = 150ml
¾ cup = 6 fluid ounces = 175ml
1 cup = 8 fluid ounces = 250ml
2 cups = 1 pint
2 pints = 1 litre
½ inch = 1 centimetre
1 inch = 2 centimetres

BAKING PAN SIZES

American	Metric
8x1½-inch round baking pan	20x4-centimetre sandwich or cake tin
9x1½-inch round baking pan	23x3.5-centimetre sandwich or cake tin
11x7x1½-inch baking pan	28x18x4-centimetre baking pan
13x9x2-inch baking pan	32.5x23x5-centimetre baking pan
2-quart rectangular baking dish	30x19x5-centimetre baking pan
15x10x1-inch baking pan	38x25.5x2.5-centimetre baking pan (Swiss roll tin)
9-inch pie plate	22x4- or 23x4-centimetre pie plate
7- or 8-inch springform pan	18- or 20-centimetre springform or loose-bottom cake tin
9x5x3-inch loaf pan	23x13x6-centimetre or 2-pound narrow loaf pan or paté tin
1½-quart casserole	1.5-litre casserole
2-quart casserole	2-litre casserole

OVEN TEMPERATURE EQUIVALENTS

Fahrenheit Setting	Celsius Setting*	Gas Setting
300°F	150°C	Gas Mark 2
325°F	160°C	Gas Mark 3
350°F	180°C	Gas Mark 4
375°F	190°C	Gas Mark 5
400°F	200°C	Gas Mark 6
425°F	220°C	Gas Mark 7
450°F	230°C	Gas Mark 8
Broil		Grill

*Electric and gas ovens may be calibrated using Celsius. However, increase the Celsius setting 10 to 20 degrees when cooking above 160°C with an electric oven. For convection or forced-air ovens (gas or electric), lower the temperature setting 10°C when cooking at all heat levels.